The Spelling Toolbox

Workbook 2

Linda Kita-Bradley

Grass Roots Press

Edmonton, Alberta, Canada

2002

The Spelling Toolbox – Workbook 2 is published by

Grass Roots Press
A division of Literacy Services of Canada Ltd.

PHONE	1-780-413-6491
FAX	1-780-413-6582
E-MAIL	info@grassrootsbooks.net
WEB	www.grassrootsbooks.net

AUTHOR	Linda Kita-Bradley
CO-ORDINATOR	Pat Campbell
EDITOR	Judith Tomlinson
COVER DESIGN	Lara Minja – Lime Design
DESIGN	Patsy Price – Far Beyond Words
LAYOUT	Patsy Price, Renate Oddy & Evelyn David – Far Beyond Words
PRINTING	Quality Color Press Inc.

ACKNOWLEDGMENT

The Word Origins were adapted from the following publication:

Hendrickson, R. (1997). *Words and phrase origins.* New York, NY: Checkmark Books.

National Library of Canada Cataloguing in Publication Data

Kita-Bradley, Linda, 1958-
        The spelling toolbox : workbook two

ISBN 978-1-894593-15-1

        1. English language—Orthography and spelling. I. Title

PE1145.2.K572 2002   428.1   C2001-903376-1

Printed in Canada

Contents

About this book

This spelling workbook aims to help adult beginner spellers develop a strategy-based approach to spelling. Although accurate spelling is the final goal, it is important that strategy building remain the focus as you and the learners work through the units in this book.

The first unit in the book introduces the five strategies, or spelling tools that the learners will use throughout the remaining twenty units. The five spelling tools are these:

- *Say, listen, and write.*
- *Make a word family.*
- *Divide and conquer.*
- *Use a spelling rule.*
- *Look for tricky parts.*

Units 2 to 21 begin with a theme-based word list followed by four parts:

■ Working with spelling tools

Learners do a series of spelling exercises that help them recognize how and when the five spelling tools can be used.

■ Trying out your spelling tools

Learners complete two dictations. The first dictation gives the learners a chance to spell the unit words as they appear in the unit word list. The second dictation manipulates the unit words in some way in order to give the learners an opportunity to choose any of the five spelling tools that can help them spell the new word. For example, if "rub" is in the unit word list, then "rubbing" or "scrub" may appear in the second dictation. Common sight words are also introduced in the second dictation.

■ Applying your spelling tools

After looking at an example, learners are asked to do a short piece of writing that relates to the unit theme. They are able to look at their spelling analytically and apply appropriate spelling tools while completing a real writing task.

■ A final word

Learners add spelling words to their personal spelling dictionary.

The workbook also includes the following:

■ Student glossary

The student glossary explains terms that the learner needs to know to complete the spelling exercises.

■ Word list

This list includes all the words that appear in the unit word lists. The list is presented alphabetically and indicates in which unit each word is found.

■ Notes for users

The notes primarily include complete dictations, word families, and explanations of the spelling rules introduced in the workbook.

■ Feature: Word Origins

The origins of various words and sayings are presented throughout the workbook. Whether or not all these stories are completely true, it is hoped that you and the learners will find them both interesting and entertaining.

introduction

unit 1

Spelling Tools

You are going to learn to use five spelling tools.
A spelling tool helps you spell words.

If you use the spelling tools in this book,
you will have a good chance
of spelling new words right . . .

and you will remember how to spell the words, too.

tool 1
Say, listen, and write.

There are many words that you can spell right if you
say the words slowly and
listen to each sound in the word.

Look at the words in the box.

cups	spots	best
thin	shot	chip
slump	grind	flunk

Say each word slowly.
Listen.
You can hear each sound.

Try it out

Say each word.
Listen to each sound.
Write the word as you say it.

spot	_spots_	pest	_chip_	
flap	_slap_	spit	_grind_	
ships	_slump_	chops	_shot_	
chimps	_cups_	craft	_slap_	

If this spelling tool does not work,
try the next spelling tool.

tool 2
Make a word family.

Words that rhyme
and have the same spelling pattern
belong to the same word family.

For example, the words **deep**, **sleep**, and **creep** rhyme.
They have the same spelling pattern: **eep**.
So, the words **deep**, **sleep**, and **creep**
belong to the word family **eep**.

Do you know a word
that rhymes with the word
you are trying to spell?

Try spelling your word the same way.

Say these pairs of words.

try fry	test chest	skirt flirt	honey money	ride slide	sick stick

Each pair of words rhymes.
Each word in the pair
is spelled the same way.

Each pair of words is a small word family.

Try it out

Say this word: **free**

Think of words that rhyme.
Write the words.

Your teacher will help you with the spelling.

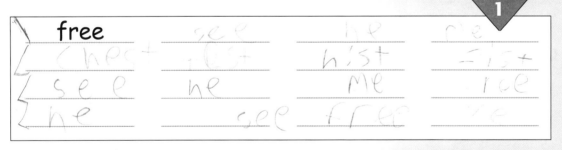

Look at your words.
Circle the words that belong to the same word family as **free**.

Learn to spell one of these words, and
you will be able to spell
all of the words.

tool 3
Divide and conquer.

If you have to spell a big word,
divide the word into parts.

Look for ❐ common beginning parts
❐ common end parts
❐ little words in the big word

Some common beginning parts		Some common end parts	
re	think – rethink	s	trap – traps
un	kind – unkind	es	bunch – bunches
dis	cover – discover	ing	bowl – bowling
pre	view – preview	ed	plant – planted
		er	drive – driver
		est	small – smallest
		ly	real – really
		y	luck – lucky
		's	his friend's car

Try it out

1— Look at the word **return**
in the box.

The beginning part is **re**.
What little word is left?

Find the beginning part
in the other words.

Divide each word.

return	<u>re turn</u>
disappear	_____
discount	_____
present	_____
rewire	_____
unlace	_____
prefab	_____

2 — Look at the word **rushes** in the box.

The end part is **es**.
What little word is left?

Find the end part in the other words.
Divide each word.

rushes	rush _____ es
talked	_____
lifting	_____
dusty	_____
grapes	_____
singer	_____
badly	_____
fastest	_____

3 — Look at the word **everyday** in the box.

What little words can you see?

Look at the other words.
Find the little words in each word.
Write the little words on the line.

everyday	every _____ day
without	_____
sometimes	_____
someone	_____
outside	_____
haircut	_____

4 — Look at the word **children** in the box.

What little word can you see?

Look at the other words.
Divide each word
by finding the little words.

children	child _____ ren
mistake	_____
flower	_____
address	_____
apartment	_____
garbage	_____

Dividing words into parts is
a good spelling tool.

But if this spelling tool does not work,
try the next spelling tool.

tool 4
Use a spelling rule.

In this book, you are going to learn four spelling rules.

The four rules are
1. The *Doubling* rule
2. The *Y* rule
3. The *Silent E* rule
4. The *Drop the E* rule

Here are some examples of each rule.

Note 2

---

1. The *Doubling* rule

fat ⟶ fatter / fattest   scrub ⟶ scrubbed / scrubby

shop⟶ shopping / shopper   glad ⟶ gladder / gladdest / gladly

---

2. The *Y* rule

marry ⟶ married / marries / marrying

study ⟶ studied / studies / studying

happy ⟶ happier / happiest / happily

stay⟶ stayed / stays / staying   buy⟶ buys / buyer / buying

---

3. The *Silent E* rule

fad / fade   slid / slide   strip / stripe

cut / cute   past / paste   scrap / scrape

---

4. The *Drop the E* rule

safe ⟶ safer / safest / safely

phone⟶ phoned / phoned / phones

move ⟶ moved / mover / moves

invite ⟶ invited / inviting / invites

You will learn more about these rules.

When you learn these rules,
    you can use them
        to help you spell many new words.

tool 5
Look for tricky parts.

Some words have tricky parts.

Say the words in the box.
Each word has a tricky part.
The tricky part is marked.

tr<u>ea</u>t	You need two letters to make the long **e** sound.
si<u>g</u>n	The letter **g** is silent.
pu<u>ll</u>	There are two **l**s in this word.
t<u>ur</u>n	The letters **ur** sound like **ir** or **er**.

How can you learn the tricky parts in a word?

Try these six steps:

1. **Read the word slowly.**

2. **Mark any tricky part.**

3. **Study the tricky part.**

4. **Cover the word.**

5. **Write the word.**

6. **Check your spelling.**

Try it out

1— Look at these words.

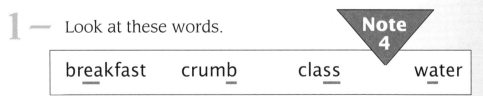

br<u>ea</u>kfast   crum<u>b</u>   clas<u>s</u>   w<u>a</u>ter

The tricky parts are marked.
Why are these parts tricky?

2— Look at the words below.
Look for the tricky parts.
Use the six steps to help you spell each word.

breakfast _____

crumb _____

class _____

water _____

treat _____

sign _____

pull _____

turn _____

Remember to . . .

1. **Read the word slowly.**
2. **Mark any tricky part.**
3. **Study the tricky part.**
4. **Cover the word.**
5. **Write the word.**
6. **Check the spelling.**

**Now you are ready
to use your new spelling tools.**

curfew

The word *curfew* comes from France.
A long time ago, people used to cook over open fires.
The open fires were in their houses.
Sometimes, the houses burned down
because the people didn't put out the fires at night.
So the French made a law.
They said people had to cover their fires at night.
Every night they rang the church bells.
The church bells reminded people to cover their fires.
The French way to say *cover fire* is *couvre feu*.
Couvre feu became the word *curfew* in English.

• word origins •

unit 2

home

Leisure

Practice words

basketball	watch	nap	late	night
afternoon	house	movie	out	early
great	quiet	order	hang	pizza

Working with spelling tools

Say, listen, and write.

Say each word.
Listen to each sound.
Write the word as you say it.

order	_____	hang	_____
quiet	_____	nap	_____

If you say these words slowly,
you will have a good chance
of spelling them right.

Make a word family.

Say this word: **out**

Think of words that rhyme.
Write the words.
Your teacher will help you with the spelling.

Note 5

out

Look at your words.
Circle the words that belong
to the same word family as **out**.

Learn to spell one of these words, and
you will be able to spell
all of the words.

Say this word: **night**

Think of words that rhyme.
Write the words.
Your teacher will help you with the spelling.

Note 6

night

Look at your words.
Circle the words that belong
to the same word family as **night**.

Learn to spell one of these words, and
you will be able to spell
all of the words.

Say this word: **noon**

Think of words that rhyme.
Write the words.
Your teacher will help you with the spelling.

Note
7

noon

Look at your words.
Circle the words that belong
to the same word family as **noon**.

Learn to spell one of these words, and
you will be able to spell
all of the words.

Say this word: **house**

Think of words that rhyme.
Write the words.
Your teacher will help you with the spelling.

Note
8

house

Look at your words.
Circle the words that belong
to the same word family as **house**.

Learn to spell one of these words, and
you will be able to spell
all of the words.

Divide and conquer.

How can you divide and conquer these words?

basketball _____

early _____

order _____

great _____

afternoon _____

Divide and conquer

Do you see
☐ common beginning parts?
☐ common end parts?
☐ little words?

Look for tricky parts.

Look at the words below.
Look for the tricky parts.
Use the six steps to help you spell the words.

watch _____

movie _____

pizza _____

late _____

Remember to...

1. **Read the word slowly.**
2. **Mark any tricky part.**
3. **Study the tricky part.**
4. **Cover the word.**
5. **Write the word.**
6. **Check the spelling.**

Trying out your spelling tools

1— Your teacher will read a paragraph. Listen. Finish the ideas.

Note 9

Use your spelling tools.

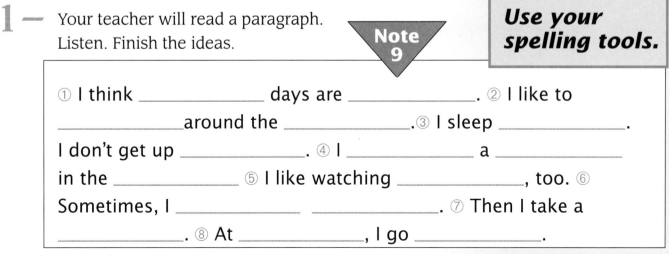

① I think _____ days are _____. ② I like to _____ around the _____. ③ I sleep _____. I don't get up _____. ④ I _____ a _____ in the _____ ⑤ I like watching _____, too. ⑥ Sometimes, I _____ _____. ⑦ Then I take a _____. ⑧ At _____, I go _____.

2— Check your spelling.
Your teacher will help you.

Which words gave you trouble?
Use a different spelling tool. Try again.

3— Your teacher will read another paragraph.
You are going to spell new words.
This will give you a chance
to try out your spelling tools.

▼ **Note 10**

> **Use your spelling tools.**
>
> **Say, listen, and write.**
>
> **Make a word family.**
>
> **Divide and conquer.**
>
> **Use a spelling rule.**
>
> **Look for tricky parts.**

① _____ _____ busy now. ② I work _____ and _____. ③ It's a _____ to stay awake.

④ I _____ these hours. ⑤ _____ _____ time to _____ this job. ⑥ I _____ go home early _____.

4— Check your spelling.
Your teacher will help you.

Which words gave you trouble?
Use a different spelling tool.
Try again.

Applying your spelling tools

1— Look at this example.

Greg has to work late.

He left a note
for his girlfriend.

Hi hon,
Can't make supper.
I have to work late.
Sorry.
How about a late movie
and pizza at my house?
Kisses,
Greggy Poo

2— Your turn.

Invite a friend
to do something.

Leave a note.

A final word

Which words about **leisure**
would you like to add
to your dictionary?

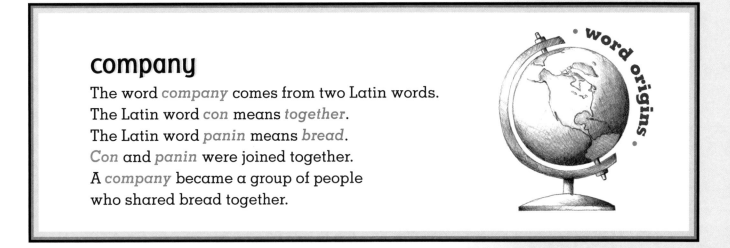

company

The word company comes from two Latin words.
The Latin word con means together.
The Latin word panin means bread.
Con and panin were joined together.
A company became a group of people
who shared bread together.

word origins

unit
3

Practice words

daughter	married	everything	fly	flat
silly	O.K.	family	hurry	took
miss	getting	trip	short	spring

Working with spelling tools

Say, listen, and write.

Say each word.
Listen to each sound.
Write the word as you say it.

O.K. _____	trip _____	flat _____
short _____	thing _____	spring _____
get _____		

If you say these words slowly,
you will have a good chance of spelling them right.

Make a word family.

Say this word: **miss**

Think of words that rhyme.
Write the words.
Your teacher will help you with the spelling.

Note 11

miss _____   _____   _____

_____   _____   _____

_____   _____   _____

Look at your words.
Circle the words that belong
to the same word family as **miss**.

Learn to spell one of these words, and
you will be able to spell
all of the words.

Say this word: **took**

Think of words that rhyme.
Write the words.
Your teacher will help you with the spelling.

Note 12

took _____   _____   _____

_____   _____   _____

_____   _____   _____

Look at your words.
Circle the words that belong
to the same word family as **took**.

Learn to spell one of these words, and
you will be able to spell
all of the words.

Say this word: **fly**

Think of words that rhyme.
Write the words.
Your teacher will help you with the spelling.

Note
13

fly _____   _____   _____   _____

_____   _____   _____   _____

_____   _____   _____   _____

Look at your words.
Circle the words that belong
to the same word family as **fly**.

Learn to spell one of these words, and
you will be able to spell
all of the word.

Divide and conquer.

How can you divide and conquer
these words?

everything _____
silly   _____

Divide and conquer

Do you see
❐ **common beginning parts?**
❐ **common end parts?**
❐ **little words?**

Use a spelling rule.

Look at these words.

get	⟶ getting
trip	⟶ tripping / tripped / tripper
flat	⟶ flatter / flattest

What happens
when you add an end part
to **get**, **trip**, and **flat**?

Practice the *Doubling* rule.

Say the base word.
Add the end part to the base word.
Say the new word.

flat + er	*flatter*
flat + est	
get + ing	
trip + ing	
trip + er	
trip + ed	
nap + ing	

> ## Doubling rule
>
> **If a word has ONE syllable and ends with ONE vowel and ONE consonant, double the final consonant when you add an end part that starts with a vowel.**

Say these words: **marry   silly   hurry   family   every**

How many syllables do you hear?

Listen to the end sound.
What sound do you hear?

Practice the *Y* rule (part 1).

Say the word.
Divide the word into two syllables.
Underline the letter that makes
the long **e** sound.

marry	*mar ry*
hurry	
every	
family	
silly	
early	

> ## Y rule (part 1)
>
> **When you hear the *long e* sound at the end of a word that has two syllables, use *y*.**
>
> **You have a good chance of being right.**

Look at these words.

marry ———►	marrying / married / marries / marriage
hurry ———►	hurrying / hurried / hurries
fly ———►	flying / flies / flier
silly ———►	silliest / sillier
family ———►	families

What happens when you add
ing to **marry**, **hurry**, and **fly**?

What happens when you add
other end parts to all the base words?

Practice the *Y* rule (part 2).

Say the base word.
Add the end part to the base word.
Say the new word.

marr**i** + ed	_married_	
marry + age	_____	
marry + ing	_____	
marry + s*	_____	
hurry + ed	_____	
hurry + ing	_____	
hurry + s*	_____	
silly + er	_____	
silly + est	_____	
early + er	_____	
early + est	_____	
family + s*	_____	
fly + s*	_____	
fly + ing	_____	
fly + er	_____	

Y rule (part 2)

If a word ends in
consonant + y,
the *y* changes to *i*
when you add all end parts
except *ing*.

* Change the **y** to **i** and add **es**.
You always need to add **es**—not only **s**—
so that the word sounds right.
Compare **marris** and **marries**,
hurris and **hurries**,
familis and **families**,
flis and **flies**.

Look for tricky parts.

Look at the words below.
Look for the tricky parts.
Use the six steps to help you
spell the words.

daughter _____
family _____
hurry _____
every _____

Remember to . . .

1. **Read the word slowly.**
2. **Mark any tricky part.**
3. **Study the tricky part.**
4. **Cover the word.**
5. **Write the word.**
6. **Check the spelling.**

Trying out your spelling tools

1— Your teacher will read a note.
Listen.
Finish the note.

Note 14

Use your spelling tools.

Say, listen, and write.

Make a word family.

Divide and conquer.

Use a spelling rule.

Look for tricky parts.

Hi Tammy,
① How is _____ with you? ② Time
sure does _____. ③ How is the
_____? ④ We had an _____
year. ⑤ Our _____ is _____
_____. ⑥ Tom and I _____
a _____ _____ in the
_____. ⑦ We had five _____
tires on the way. ⑧ We felt pretty
_____. ⑨ _____ up and
write! ⑩ We _____ you.
            Love,
            Brenda and Tom

2— Check your spelling.
Your teacher will help you.

Which words gave you trouble?
Use a different spelling tool.
Try again.

3— Your teacher will read another note.
You are going to spell new words.
This will give you a chance
to try out your spelling tools.

Note 15

Use your spelling tools.

Say, listen, and write.

Make a word family.

Divide and conquer.

Use a spelling rule.

Look for tricky parts.

Hi guys!

① *You're right. Time really _____.* ② *The years seem to _____ _____.* ③ *I feel like _____ _____ all the time.*

④ *How are the _____ plans going?*
⑤ *_____ sister _____ on the ice.* ⑥ *_____ hurt _____ _____.* ⑦ *_____ staying _____ _____ now.*

⑧ *Anyway, watch out for _____!* ⑨ *Hope to see you sometime _____.*

Tammy

Check your spelling.
Your teacher will help you.

Which words gave you trouble?
Use a different spelling tool.
Try again.

Applying your spelling tools

1— Look at this example.

Vicky sends her friend
a birthday card.

She writes
a short note inside.

> Happy Birthday, Mona!
>
> Hope everything is O.K.
> with you.
>
> Lenny retired in the spring.
> I'm still working. We hope to
> have a short winter. We're
> getting lots of snow this year.
>
> Have a good year!
> Vicky

2— Your turn.

Write
a Christmas note
to a friend.

A final word

Which words about **family times**
would you like to add
to your dictionary?

Practice words

stuff	save	money	pens	books
notebook	binders	picky	lined	paper
clothes	runners	erasers	fussy	rulers

Working with spelling tools

Say, listen, and write.

Say each word.
Listen to each sound.
Write the word as you say it.

pen _____	binder _____	paper _____
eraser_____	ruler _____	cloth _____
run _____		

If you say these words slowly,
you will have a good chance of spelling them right.

Make a word family.

Say this word: **book**

Think of words that rhyme.
Write the words.
Your teacher will help you with the spelling.

Note 16

book	_____	_____
_____	_____	_____
_____	_____	_____

Look at your words.
Circle the words that belong
to the same word family as **book**.

Learn to spell one of these words, and
you will be able to spell
all of the words.

Say this word: **pick**

Think of words that rhyme.
Write the words.
Your teacher will help you with the spelling.

Note 17

pick	_____	_____
_____	_____	_____
_____	_____	_____
_____	_____	_____

Look at your words.
Circle the words that belong
to the same word family as **pick**.

Learn to spell one of these words, and
you will be able to spell all of the words.

Divide and conquer.

How can you divide and conquer these words?

pens	_____
binders	_____
erasers	_____
books	_____
picky	_____
clothes	_____
fussy	_____
notebooks	_____
rulers	_____

Divide and conquer

Do you see
- ☐ common beginning parts?
- ☐ common end parts?
- ☐ little words?

Use a spelling rule.

Practice the *Doubling* rule.

Say the base word.
Add the end part to the base word.
Say the new word.

run + ing	_____
run + er	_____
run + s	_____
run + y	_____
pen + y	_____
pen + s	_____

Doubling rule

If a word has ONE syllable and ends with ONE vowel and ONE consonant, double the final consonant when you add an end part that starts with a vowel.

Practice the *Y* rule (part 1).

Say the word.
Divide the word into two syllables.
Underline the letter that makes
the long **e** sound.

picky _____
fussy _____
penny _____
runny _____

Practice the *Y* rule (part 2).

Say the base word.
Add the end part to the base word.
Say the new word.

picky + er _____
picky + est _____
penny + s _____
fussy + er _____
fussy + est _____

Read the plural word.
Does it sound right?

Y rule (part 1)

**When you hear
the *long e* sound
at the end of a word
that has two syllables,
use *y*.**

**You have a good chance
of being right.**

Y rule (part 2)

**If a word ends in
consonant + y,
the *y* changes to *i*
when you add all end parts
except *ing*.**

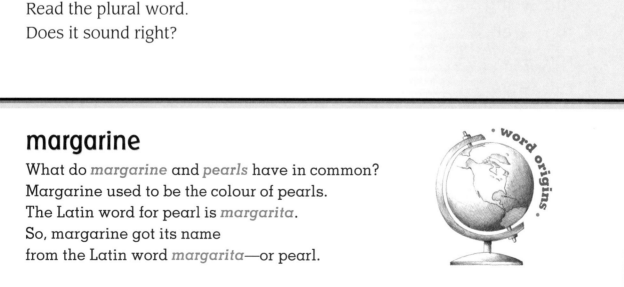

margarine

What do *margarine* and *pearls* have in common?
Margarine used to be the colour of pearls.
The Latin word for pearl is *margarita*.
So, margarine got its name
from the Latin word *margarita*—or pearl.

· word origins ·

Your teacher will read these pairs of words.
Listen.

not	cloth	strip	Sid
note	clothe	stripe	side

What happens to the short vowel sound in a word
when you add **e** to the end of the word?

Practice the *Silent E* rule

Say the base word.
Add the letter **e**. Say the new word.

> **Silent E rule**
>
> **When you add the letter *e*
> to the end of a word,
> the short vowel sound
> in that word changes to
> a long vowel sound.**

not	+ e	_note_
grip	+ e	
strip	+ e	
grim	+ e	
Sid	+ e	
cop	+ e	
cloth	+ e	
scrap	+ e	

Look at the words below.
What happens when you add **ed**, **ing** or **er**?

erase	⟶	erased / erasing / eraser
save	⟶	saved / saving / saver
rule	⟶	ruled / ruling / ruler

Practice the *Drop the E* rule.

Say the base word.
Cross out the silent **e**.
Add the end part to the base word.

save + ed	_saved_	
save + er	_____	
save + ing	_____	
erase + ed	_____	
erase + ing	_____	
erase + er	_____	clothe + ing _____
note + ed	_____	rule + ed _____
note + ing	_____	rule + er _____
line + ing	_____	rule + ing _____
line + er	_____	late + er _____
line + ed	_____	late + est _____

Look for tricky parts.

Look at the words below.
Look for the tricky parts.
Use the six steps to help you spell the words.

Remember to . . .

1. Read the word slowly.
2. Mark any tricky part.
3. Study the tricky part.
4. Cover the word.
5. Write the word.
6. Check the spelling.

stuff	_____
clothes	_____
money	_____
fuss	_____

Trying out your spelling tools

1 — Your teacher will read a paragraph.
Listen. Finish the ideas.

Note 18

① School _____ is pretty expensive.
② I really have to _____ my
_____. ③ My kids need
_____ and _____. ④ They
need _____ and _____. ⑤ They need
_____ and _____. ⑥ They need tons of
_____ _____. ⑦ They always need new
_____. ⑧ Things like _____ aren't cheap.
⑨ And kids are so _____ and _____.

Use your spelling tools.

Say, listen, and write.

Make a word family.

Divide and conquer.

Use a spelling rule.

Look for tricky parts.

2 — Check your spelling.
Your teacher will help you.

Which words gave you trouble?
Use a different spelling tool. Try again.

3 — Your teacher will read a shopping list.
You are going to spell new words.
This will give you a chance to try out your spelling tools.

Note 19

① _____ shoes
② _____
③ white _____ stuff
④ bathroom _____
⑤ _____ foam
⑥ _____ and _____ paper

Use your spelling tools.

Say, listen, and write.

Make a word family.

Divide and conquer.

Use a spelling rule.

Look for tricky parts.

4 — Check your spelling.
Your teacher will help you.

Which words gave you trouble?
Use a different spelling tool. Try again.

Applying your spelling tools

1— Look at this example.

Tina's kids need stuff for school.

This is Tina's shopping list.

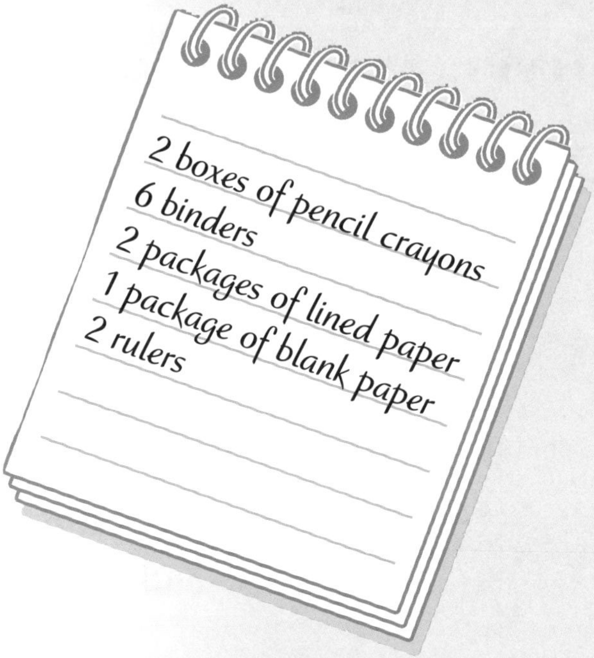

2 boxes of pencil crayons
6 binders
2 packages of lined paper
1 package of blank paper
2 rulers

2— Your turn.

Your kids need
stuff for school.

Write your shopping list.

A final word

Which words about *shopping*
would you like to add
to your dictionary?

Practice words

apartment	knock	add	repaper	close*
outside	painting	kitchen	switches	strip
varnish	table	retile	floor	hire

*as in *I live close to the sea.*

Working with spelling tools

Say, listen, and write.

Say each word.
Listen to each sound.
Write the word as you say it.

repaper	_____	strip	_____
part	_____	varnish	_____

If you say these words slowly,
you will have a good chance of spelling them right.

Make a word family.

Say this word: **knock**

Think of words that rhyme.
Write the words.
Your teacher will help you with the spelling.

Note 20

knock _____ _____

_____ _____ _____

_____ _____ _____

_____ _____ _____

Look at your words.
Circle the words that belong
to the same word family as **knock**.

Learn to spell one of these words, and
you will be able to spell
all of the words.

Say this word: **paint**

Think of words that rhyme.
Write the words.
Your teacher will help you with the spelling.

Note 21

paint _____ _____

_____ _____ _____

_____ _____ _____

Look at your words.
Circle the words that belong
to the same word family as **paint**.

Learn to spell one of these words, and
you will be able to spell
all of the words.

Say this word: **switch**

Think of words that rhyme.
Write the words.
Your teacher will help you with the spelling.

switch _____ _____

_____ _____ _____

_____ _____ _____

Look at your words.
Circle the words that belong
to the same word family as **switch**.

Learn to spell one of these words, and
you will be able to spell
all of the words.

Say this word: **table**

Think of words that rhyme.
Write the words.
Your teacher will help you with the spelling. Note 23

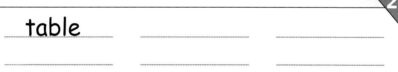

table _____ _____

_____ _____ _____

_____ _____ _____

Look at your words.
Circle the words that belong
to the same word family as **table**.

Learn to spell one of these words, and
you will be able to spell
all of the words.

Divide and conquer.

How can you divide and conquer these words?

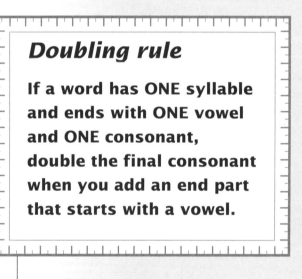

Divide and conquer

Do you see
- ☐ **common beginning parts?**
- ☐ **common end parts?**
- ☐ **little words?**

apartment _____

repaper _____

painting _____

retile _____

outside _____

switches _____

Use a spelling rule.

Practice the *Doubling* rule.

Say the base word.
Add the end part to the base word.
Say the new word.

strip + ing _____

strip + ed _____

strip + s _____

strip + er _____

Doubling rule

If a word has ONE syllable and ends with ONE vowel and ONE consonant, double the final consonant when you add an end part that starts with a vowel.

Practice the *Silent E* rule.

Say the word.
Underline the long vowel sound.
Circle the silent **e**.

| hire | side |
| tile | close |

Silent E rule

When you add the letter *e* to the end of a word, the short vowel sound in that word changes to a long vowel sound.

Practice the *Drop the E* rule.

Say the base word.
Add the end part to the base word.
Say the new word.

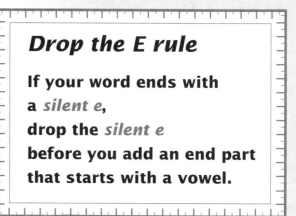

Drop the E rule

If your word ends with
a *silent e*,
drop the *silent e*
before you add an end part
that starts with a vowel.

hire + ed _____

hire + ing _____

hire + s _____

side + ing _____

side + s _____

retile + ed _____

tile + s _____

retile + ing _____

close + er _____

close + est _____

close + ly _____

table + s _____

Look for tricky parts.

Look at the words below.
Look for the tricky parts.
Use the six steps to help you
spell the words.

Remember to...

1. **Read the word slowly.**

2. **Mark any tricky part.**

3. **Study the tricky part.**

4. **Cover the word.**

5. **Write the word.**

6. **Check the spelling.**

outside _____

add _____

floor _____

knock _____

kitchen _____

Trying out your spelling tools

1 — Your teacher will read a letter.
Listen. Finish the ideas.

Note 24

Hi Val,

① I rented that _____. ② I'm _____ to a mall.
③ The _____ hall needs _____. ④ I have to wire
the _____. ⑤ I want to _____ out a wall.
⑥ I want to _____ a fireplace. ⑦ I want to _____
the _____. ⑧ I want to _____ and _____
the _____. ⑨ I want to _____ someone to
_____ the _____.
What do you think?
Mitch

2 — Check your spelling.
Your teacher will help you.

Which words gave you trouble?
Use a different spelling tool. Try again.

3 — Your teacher will read another letter.
You are going to spell new words.
This will give you a chance
to try out your spelling tools.

Note 25

Use your spelling tools.

Say, listen, and write.

Make a word family.

Divide and conquer.

Use a spelling rule.

Look for tricky parts.

Hi Mitch,

① _____ a fireplace! Wow! ② I have _____ before.
③ _____ messy work. ④ I have _____ and
_____ _____. ⑤ _____ good at it
_____. ⑥ _____ somebody is a _____
idea. ⑦ _____ about me? ⑧ _____ does the
landlord think _____ _____ this?
Val

4— Check your spelling.
Your teacher will help you.

Which words gave you trouble?
Use a different spelling tool. Try again.

Applying your spelling tools

1— Look at this example.

Vinit wants to fix up his apartment.
He writes a note
to the building manager.

Is it O.K. if I paint the
kitchen and repaper the
bathroom?
Also, my hall light
doesn't work.
Can you check it out?

Vinit
Apt. 808

2— Your turn.

Think about your place.
Would you like to fix it up
in some way?

Write a note
to the building manager.

A final word

Which words about *fix it up*
would you like to add
to your dictionary?

unit
6

home
Changes

Practice words

stairs	elevator	address	lease	because
heating	damage	deposit	brighter	basement
good-bye	washer	drier	cleaner	bigger

Working with spelling tools

Say, listen, and write.

Say each word.
Listen to each sound.
Write the word as you say it.

deposit _____ washer _____ big_____

If you say these words slowly,
you will have a good chance
of spelling them right.

Make a word family.

Say this word: **clean**

Think of words that rhyme.
Write the words.
Your teacher will help you with the spelling.

Note 26

clean		

Look at your words.
Circle the words that belong to the same word family as **clean**.

Learn to spell one of these words, and
you will be able to spell all of the words.

Say this word: **bright**

Think of words that rhyme.
Write the words.
Your teacher will help you with the spelling.

Note 27

bright		

Look at your words.
Circle the words that belong to the same word family as **bright**.

Learn to spell one of these words, and
you will be able to spell all of the words.

Say this word: **heat**

Think of words that rhyme.
Write the words.
Your teacher will help you with the spelling.

Note
28

heat _____ _____ _____

_____ _____ _____

_____ _____ _____

_____ _____ _____

_____ _____ _____

Look at your words.
Circle the words that belong to the same word family as **heat**.

Learn to spell one of these words, and
you will be able to spell all of the words.

Divide and conquer.

How can you divide and conquer
these words?

stairs _____

damage _____

basement _____

elevator _____

because _____

deposit _____

good-bye _____

cleaner _____

address _____

heating _____

brighter _____

washer _____

Divide and conquer

Do you see
- ❑ **common beginning parts?**
- ❑ **common end parts?**
- ❑ **little words?**

Use a spelling rule.

Practice the *Doubling* rule.

Say the base word.
Add the end part to the base word.
Say the new word.

big + est _____
big + er _____

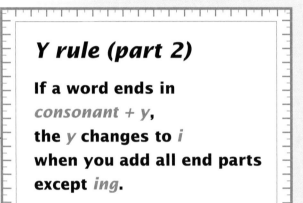

Doubling rule

If a word has ONE syllable and ends with ONE vowel and ONE consonant, double the final consonant when you add an end part that starts with a vowel.

Practice the *Y* rule (part 2).

Say the base word.
Add the end part to the base word.
Say the new word.

dry + er _____
dry + ed _____
dry + ing _____
dry + s _____

Y rule (part 2)

If a word ends in
consonant + y,
the *y* changes to *i*
when you add all end parts
except *ing*.

Read the last word.
Does it sound right?

Practice the *Silent E* rule.

Say the word.
Underline the long vowel sound.
Circle the silent **e**.

base   elevate

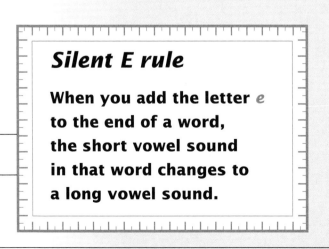

Silent E rule

When you add the letter *e*
to the end of a word,
the short vowel sound
in that word changes to
a long vowel sound.

Practice the *Drop the E* rule.

Say the base word.
Add the end part to the base word.
Say the new word.

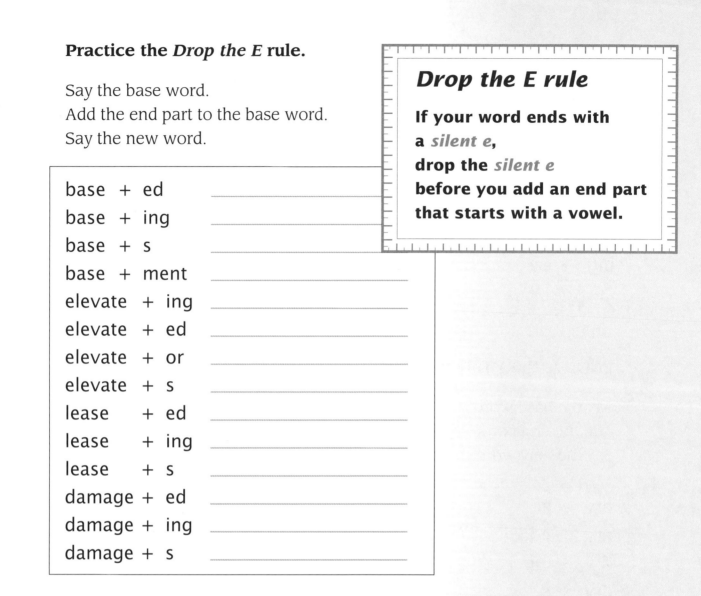

Drop the E rule

If your word ends with
a *silent e*,
drop the *silent e*
before you add an end part
that starts with a vowel.

base + ed _____

base + ing _____

base + s _____

base + ment _____

elevate + ing _____

elevate + ed _____

elevate + or _____

elevate + s _____

lease + ed _____

lease + ing _____

lease + s _____

damage + ed _____

damage + ing _____

damage + s _____

Look for tricky parts.

Look at the words below.
Look for the tricky parts.
Use the six steps to help you
spell the words.

Remember to...

1. Read the word slowly.

2. Mark any tricky part.

3. Study the tricky part.

4. Cover the word.

5. Write the word.

6. Check the spelling.

friend _____

park _____

tea _____

weekend _____

Trying out your spelling tools

1— Your teacher will read a letter to the building manager.
Listen. Finish the ideas.

Note 29

Dear Manager,

① I need to break my _____ _____ this place is
_____ cold. ② I don't expect my _____
_____ back. ③ My new place is _____,
_____, and _____. ④ The _____ works.
⑤ So, _____ _____. ⑥ There's a _____
and _____ in the _____. ⑦ The _____
works. ⑧ I'm happy I have a new _____!

            Clair Tomlin
            Apt. 8

2— Check your spelling.
Your teacher will help you.

Which words gave you trouble?
Use a different spelling tool. Try again.

3— Your teacher will read a letter
to the manager of the new apartment.
You are going to spell new words.
This will give you a chance to try out your spelling tools.

Use your spelling tools.

Say, listen, and write.

Make a word family.

Divide and conquer.

Use a spelling rule.

Look for tricky parts.

Note 30

Dear Manager,

① _____ apartment is not good. ② I spent _____
weeks _____ it. ③ The elevator is still _____.
④ I have to climb ten _____ of stairs! ⑤ I _____ to
buy a _____. ⑥ The floors _____ _____.
⑦ The _____ is full of water. ⑧ What a _____!
_____ me! ⑨ I was better off _____ my old place.

            Clair Tomlin
            Apt. 2

4 — Check your spelling.
Your teacher will help you.

Which words gave you trouble?
Use a different spelling tool. Try again.

Applying your spelling tools

1 — Look at this example.

Stan needs to move.

He gives the building manager notice.

Our lease is up in two months. We are moving at that time be-cause my wife is pregnant. We need a bigger place. When can we expect the damage deposit?

Sincerely,
Stan Diller
Stan Diller, Apt. 34

2 — Your turn.

You are moving.

Give notice.
Give a reason.

A final word

Which words about **home changes**
would you like to add to your dictionary?

Practice words

something	local	hobby	interests	happening
groups	radio	listen	favourite	newspaper
belong	join	always	area	centre

Working with spelling tools

Say, listen, and write.

Say each word.
Listen to each sound.
Write the word as you say it.

long _____	thing _____	paper _____

If you say these words slowly,
you will have a good chance
of spelling them right.

Divide and conquer.

How can you divide and conquer these words?

something _____
interests _____
newspaper _____
happening _____
belong _____
listen _____
favourite _____
always _____
groups _____

Divide and conquer

Do you see
❐ **common beginning parts?**
❐ **common end parts?**
❐ **little words?**

Use a spelling rule.

Practice the *Y* rule (part 1).

Say the word.
Divide the word into syllables.
Underline the letter that makes
the long **e** sound.

hobby _____

Practice the *Y* rule (part 2).

Say the base word.
Add the end part to the base word.
Say the new word.

hobby + s _____

Does the new word sound right?

Y rule (part 1)

**When you hear
the *long e* sound
at the end of a word
that has two syllables,
use *y*.**

**You have a good chance
of being right.**

Y rule (part 2)

**If a word ends in
consonant + y,
the *y* changes to *i*
when you add all end parts
except *ing*.**

Practice the *Drop the E* rule.

Say the base word.
Add the end part to the base word.
Say thc new word.

centre + ed   _____

centre + ing   _____

centre + s   _____

favourite + s   _____

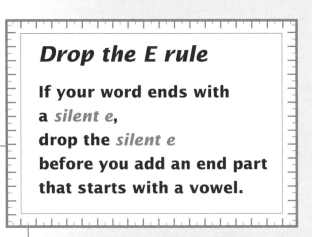

Drop the E rule

**If your word ends with
a *silent e*,
drop the *silent e*
before you add an end part
that starts with a vowel.**

Look for tricky parts.

Look at the words below.
Look for the tricky parts.
Use the six steps to help you
spell the words.

Remember to . . .

1. **Read the word slowly.**

2. **Mark any tricky part.**

3. **Study the tricky part.**

4. **Cover the word.**

5. **Write the word.**

6. **Check the spelling.**

some   _____

interest   _____

radio   _____

news   _____

local   _____

happen   _____

listen   _____

area   _____

group   _____

favourite _____

join   _____

centre   _____

Trying out your spelling tools

1 — Your teacher will read a paragraph.
Listen.
Finish the ideas.

Note 31

What's happening in your town? ① Do you have a _____
_____? ② What are your _____? ③ Do you
_____ to any _____? ④ _____ a
_____ rec _____. ⑤ Check the _____.
⑥ _____ to the _____. ⑦ They tell you what's
_____ in your _____. ⑧ There's _____
_____ to do.

2 — Check your spelling.
Your teacher will help you.

Which words gave you trouble?
Use a different spelling tool. Try again.

3 — Your teacher will read another paragraph.
You are going to spell new words.
This will give you a chance
to try out your spelling tools.

Note 32

> ***Use your spelling tools.***
>
> **Say, listen, and write.**
>
> **Make a word family.**
>
> **Divide and conquer.**
>
> **Use a spelling rule.**
>
> **Look for tricky parts.**

① My _____ loves movies. ② He _____ a
_____ _____. ③ _____ _____
it! ④ He _____ it's very _____. ⑤ _____
go on trips _____. ⑥ Maybe _____ join the club.
⑦ I don't have _____ _____. ⑧ _____
anyone _____ watch a movie.

4 — Check your spelling.
Your teacher will help you.

Which words gave you trouble?
Use a different spelling tool. Try again.

Applying your spelling tools

1— Look at this example.

Saul gets this form
in the mail.
It's from the
community centre.

He fills it out.

We are planning new programs for next year.
What are your favourite hobbies or interests?
fishing
watching movies

What kinds of groups would you like to join?
darts club
movie club
running club

Thanks for your help!
See you at the centre next year.

We are planning new programs for next year.
What are your favourite hobbies or interests?

What kinds of groups would you like to join?

Thanks for your help!
See you at the centre next year.

2— Your turn.

What do you
like to do?

Fill out this form
from your
community centre.

A final word

Which words about **things to do**
would you like to add
to your dictionary?

unit 8

community Action

Practice words

person	feel	acts	friendly	problem
word	kind	saying	smile	simple
someone	around	easy	others	helping

Working with spelling tools

Say, listen, and write.

Say each word.
Listen to each sound.
Write the word as you say it.

kind _____	helping _____	act _____

If you say these words slowly,
you will have a good chance
of spelling them right.

Make a word family.

Say this word: **round**

Think of words that rhyme.
Write the words.
Your teacher will help you with the spelling.

Note 33

round		

Look at your words.
Circle the words that belong
to the same word family as **round**.

Learn to spell one of these words, and
you will be able to spell
all of the words.

Say this word: **simple**

Think of words that rhyme.
Write the words.
Your teacher will help you with the spelling.

Note 34

simple		

Look at your words.
Circle the words that belong
to the same word family as **simple**.

Learn to spell one of these words, and
you will be able to spell
all of the words.

Say this word: **feel**

Think of words that rhyme.
Write the words.
Your teacher will help you with the spelling.

Note 35

feel _____ _____
_____ _____ _____
_____ _____ _____
_____ _____ _____
_____ _____ _____

Look at your words.
Circle the words that belong
to the same word family as **feel**.

Learn to spell one of these words, and
you will be able to spell
all of the words.

Say this word: **other**

Think of words that rhyme.
Write the words.
Your teacher will help you with the spelling.

Note 36

other _____ _____
_____ _____ _____
_____ _____ _____

Look at your words.
Circle the words that belong
to the same word family as **other**.

Learn to spell one of these words, and
you will be able to spell
all of the words.

Divide and conquer.

How can you divide and conquer these words?

person _____

friendly _____

saying _____

someone _____

others _____

acts _____

around _____

helping _____

Divide and conquer

Do you see
- ❐ **common beginning parts?**
- ❐ **common end parts?**
- ❐ **little words?**

Use a spelling rule.

Practice the *Y* rule (part 1).

Say the word.
Divide the word into two syllables.
Underline the letter that makes the long **e** sound.

easy _____

Y rule (part 1)

When you hear the *long e* sound at the end of a word that has two syllables, use *y*.

You have a good chance of being right.

· **word origins** ·

IOU

The term *IOU* is four hundred years old. *IOU* stands for *I Owe You*.

Practice the *Y* rule (part 2).

Say the base word.
Add the end part to the base word.
Say the new word.

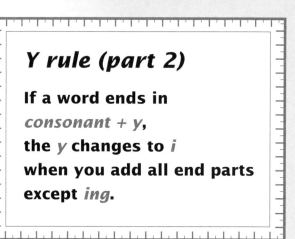

Y rule (part 2)

If a word ends in
consonant + y,
the *y* changes to *i*
when you add all end parts
except *ing.*

easy + er	_____
easy + est	_____
easy + ly	_____
friendly + er	_____
friendly + est	_____
say + s	_____
say + ing	_____

The **Y** rule doesn't apply to some of these words.
Which ones are they?
Why doesn't the rule apply?

Practice the *Silent E* rule.

Say the word.
Underline
the long vowel sound.
Circle the letter **e**.

Silent E rule

When you add the letter *e*
to the end of a word,
the short vowel sound in that word
changes to a long vowel sound.

smile

Practice the *Drop the E* rule.

Say the base word.
Add the end part to the base word.
Say the new word.

Drop the E rule

If your word ends with
a *silent e,*
drop the *silent e*
before you add an end part
that starts with a vowel.

smile + ed	_____
smile + ing	_____
smile + s	_____

Look for tricky parts.

Look at the words below.
Look for the tricky parts.
Use the six steps to help you
spell the words.

some _____
one _____
easy _____
word _____
friend _____
problem _____

Remember to...

1. **Read the word slowly.**
2. **Mark any tricky part.**
3. **Study the tricky part.**
4. **Cover the word.**
5. **Write the word.**
6. **Check the spelling.**

Trying out your spelling tools

1— Your teacher will read a paragraph.
Listen.
Finish the ideas.

Note 37

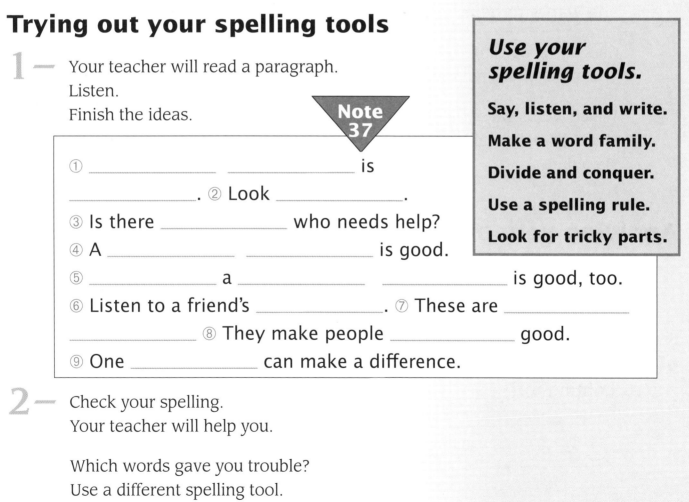

① _____ _____ is
_____. ② Look _____.
③ Is there _____ who needs help?
④ A _____ _____ is good.
⑤ _____ a _____ _____ is good, too.
⑥ Listen to a friend's _____. ⑦ These are _____
_____ ⑧ They make people _____ good.
⑨ One _____ can make a difference.

Use your spelling tools.

Say, listen, and write.

Make a word family.

Divide and conquer.

Use a spelling rule.

Look for tricky parts.

2— Check your spelling.
Your teacher will help you.

Which words gave you trouble?
Use a different spelling tool.
Try again.

3 — Your teacher will read another paragraph.
You are going to spell new words.
This will give you a chance
to try out your spelling tools.

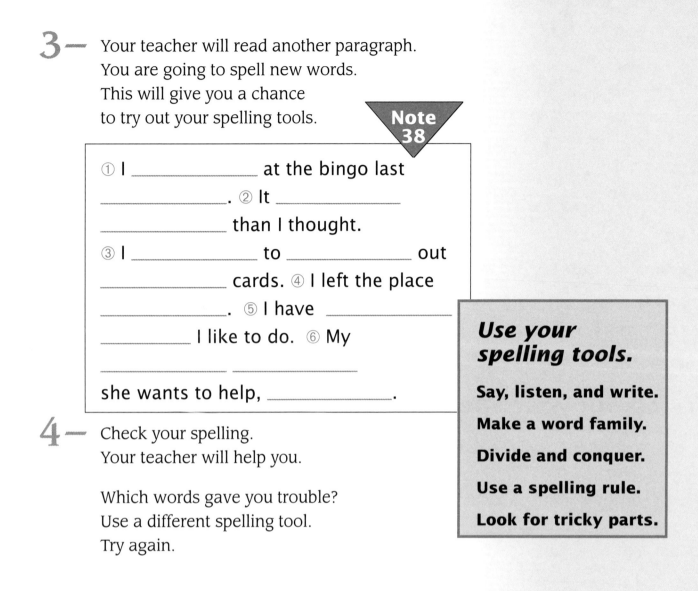

▼ **Note 38**

① I _____ at the bingo last
_____. ② It _____
_____ than I thought.
③ I _____ to _____ out
_____ cards. ④ I left the place
_____. ⑤ I have _____
_____ I like to do. ⑥ My
_____ _____
she wants to help, _____.

Use your spelling tools.

Say, listen, and write.

Make a word family.

Divide and conquer.

Use a spelling rule.

Look for tricky parts.

4 — Check your spelling.
Your teacher will help you.

Which words gave you trouble?
Use a different spelling tool.
Try again.

Applying your spelling tools

1 — Look at this example.

Here is a poster.

What is the community
fighting for?

Help Save our Park!
We don't need another parking lot!
Come to the meeting.
Bring a friend.

Place: Local Community Centre
Date: November 8
Time: 8:00 p.m.

Do it for your children.

2— Your turn.

What does your community need?

Make a poster.

A final word

Which words about *community action* would you like to add to your dictionary?

unit
9

Practice words

children	rich	forget	strong	place
very	adults	ministers	police	teachers
parents	lucky	healthy	let's	members

Working with spelling tools

Say, listen, and write.

Say each word. Listen to each sound.
Write the word as you say it.

child _____	strong _____	adult _____
rich _____	minister _____	member _____
let _____		

If you say these words slowly,
you will have a good chance
of spelling them right.

Make a word family.

Say this word: **teach**

Think of words that rhyme.
Write the words.
Your teacher will help you with the spelling.

Note 39

> teach _____   _____
>
> _____   _____   _____
>
> _____   _____   _____

Look at your words.
Circle the words that belong
to the same word family as **teach**.

Learn to spell one of these words, and
you will be able to spell all of the words.

Say this word: **luck**

Think of words that rhyme.
Write the words.
Your teacher will help you with the spelling.

Note 40

> luck _____   _____
>
> _____   _____   _____
>
> _____   _____   _____
>
> _____   _____   _____
>
> _____   _____   _____

Look at your words.
Circle the words that belong
to the same word family as **luck**.

Learn to spell one of these words, and
you will be able to spell
all of the words.

Say this word: **place**

Think of words that rhyme.
Write the words.
Your teacher will help you with the spelling.

Note 41

place		

Look at your words.
Circle the words that belong
to the same word family as **place**.

Learn to spell one of these words, and
you will be able to spell
all of the words.

Divide and conquer.

How can you divide and conquer
these words?

children _____

teachers _____

healthy _____

parents _____

forget _____

police _____

lucky _____

members _____

adults _____

let's _____

Divide and conquer

Do you see
☐ **common beginning parts?**
☐ **common end parts?**
☐ **little words?**

Use a spelling rule.

Practice the *Y* rule (part 1).

Say the word.
Divide the word into two syllables.
Underline the letter that makes
the long **e** sound.

healthy	_____
lucky	_____
very	_____

Practice the *Y* rule (part 2).

Say the base word.
Add the end part to the base word.
Say the new word.

healthy + er	_____
healthy + est	_____
lucky + er	_____
lucky + est	_____
lucky + ly	_____

Y rule (part 1)

**When you hear
the *long e* sound
at the end of a word
that has two syllables,
use *y*.**

**You have a good chance
of being right.**

Y rule (part 2)

**If a word ends in
consonant + y,
the *y* changes to *i*
when you add all end parts
except *ing*.**

Practice the *Silent E* rule.

Say the word.
Underline the long vowel sound.
Circle the silent **e**.

place

Silent E rule

**When you add the letter *e*
to the end of a word,
the short vowel sound
in that word changes to
a long vowel sound.**

Practice the *Drop the E* rule.

Say the base word.
Add the end part to the base word.
Say the new word

place + ed	_____
place + ing	_____
place + s	_____
police + ed	_____
police + ing	_____
police + s	_____

Drop the E rule

**If your word ends with
a *silent e*,
drop the *silent e*
before you add an end part
that starts with a vowel.**

Look for tricky parts.

Look at the words below.
Look for the tricky parts.
Use the six steps to help you
spell the words.

health	_____
very	_____

Remember to . . .

1. **Read the word slowly.**
2. **Mark any tricky part.**
3. **Study the tricky part.**
4. **Cover the word.**
5. **Write the word.**
6. **Check the spelling.**

word origins

alive and kicking

People used to buy fish from fish sellers.
The people wanted fresh fish.
The fish sellers used to say:
"Look how fresh my fish is.
It is still alive and kicking."
Today, *alive and kicking* means *active*.

Trying out your spelling tools

1— Your teacher will read part of a newsletter.
Listen.
Finish the newsletter.

Note 42

Dear Community Readers,

① We have a _____, _____ community.

② I thank many community _____ for this.

    ③ ▪ Our _____ and our _____.

    ④ ▪ Our _____ and our_____.

    ⑤ ▪ Our _____ and young _____.

⑥ We're _____ _____. ⑦ Let's not

_____ how _____ we are. ⑧ _____

keep this a great _____ to live.

                    Andrew Dobbs, Editor

2— Check your spelling.
Your teacher will help you.

Which words gave you trouble?
Use a different spelling tool. Try again.

3— Your teacher will read part of a newsletter again.
You are going to spell new words.
This will give you a chance
to try out your spelling tools.

Note 43

Use your spelling tools.

Say, listen, and write.

Make a word family.

Divide and conquer.

Use a spelling rule.

Look for tricky parts.

Dear Community Readers,

① We are losing a _____ of _____community.

② Carmen Chen is off to new _____. ③ _____

going to Africa to _____. ④ _____ miss her.

⑤ Our community is _____ because of _____.

⑥ Don't stay _____ too _____, Carmen!

⑦ Best _____ _____ us all.

                    Andrew Dobbs, Editor

---

4 — Check your spelling.
Your teacher will help you.

Which words gave you trouble?
Use a different spelling tool.
Try again.

Applying your spelling tools

1 — Look at this example.

May Smith wants
to say "Thank you."

She writes a note
to the community newletter.

Dear Readers,

I would like to thank Dave Evans.
He clears my sidewalk from snow.
He never forgets.
I'm very lucky he's my neighbour.
Thank you, Dave.

May Smith

hijack

In the 1930s, you couldn't sell alcohol.
Selling alcohol was against the law.
Some people sold alcohol anyway.
They carried the alcohol in trucks.
Crooks used to rob the trucks.
The crooks would say to the truck drivers,
"Stick 'em up high, Jack."
People started to call the crooks *highjackers*.
That's how we got the words
hijack and *hijacker*.

word origins

2 — Your turn.

Send a message to someone.
Write to your community newsletter.

> **Dear Readers,**
>
> _____
> _____
> _____
> _____
> _____
> _____
> _____
> _____
> _____
> _____
> _____
> _____

A final word

Which words about **community relations**
would you like to add
to your dictionary?

Christmas carol

Carole means *ring* in French.
Christmas singers used to dance in a ring
as they sang Christmas songs.
Now, Christmas songs are called *Christmas carols*.

unit 10

community

Changes

Practice words

trust	accept	alone	open	understand
arms	stand	minds	jobs	true
closed	facts	story	tell	nobody

Working with spelling tools

Say, listen, and write.

Say each word.
Listen to each sound.
Write the word as you say it.

open	_____	stand	_____	trust	_____
mind	_____	arm	_____	job	_____
fact	_____	understand	_____		

If you say these words slowly,
you will have a good chance of spelling them right.

Make a word family.

Say this word: **tell**

Think of words that rhyme.
Write the words.
Your teacher will help you with the spelling.

Note
44

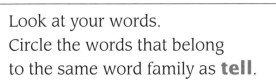

tell _____   _____

_____   _____   _____

_____   _____   _____

Look at your words.
Circle the words that belong
to the same word family as **tell**.

Learn to spell one of these words, and
you will be able to spell
all of the words.

Divide and conquer.

How can you divide and conquer
these words?

open   _____
understand_____
minds   _____
nobody   _____
alone   _____
arms   _____
jobs   _____
facts   _____

> ### *Divide and conquer*
>
> **Do you see**
> ☐ **common beginning parts?**
> ☐ **common end parts?**
> ☐ **little words?**

Use a spelling rule.

Practice the *Y* rule (part 1).

Say the word.
Divide the word into two syllables.
Underline the letter that
makes the long **e** sound.

body	_____
story	_____

Practice the *Y* rule (part 2).

Say the base word.
Add the end part to the base word.
Say the new word.

body + s	_____
story + s	_____

Say each word.
Does it sound right?

Practice the *Silent E* rule.

Say the word.
Underline the long vowel sound.
Circle the silent **e**.

close	alone

> ### *Y rule (part 1)*
>
> **When you hear
> the *long e* sound
> at the end of a word
> that has two syllables,
> use *y*.**
>
> **You have a good chance
> of being right.**
>
> ### *Y rule (part 2)*
>
> **If a word ends in
> *consonant + y*,
> the *y* changes to *i*
> when you add all end parts
> except *ing*.**

> ### *Silent E rule*
>
> **When you add the letter *e*
> to the end of a word,
> the short vowel sound
> in that word changes to
> a long vowel sound.**

Practice the *Drop the E* rule.

Say the base word.
Add the end part to the base word.
Say the new word.

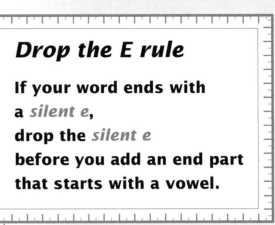

Drop the E rule

**If your word ends with
a *silent e*,
drop the *silent e*
before you add an end part
that starts with a vowel.**

close + ed	_____
close + ing	_____
close + s	_____
lone + er	_____
lone + ly	_____
true + ly*	_____
true + est	_____
true + er	_____

*Truly is an exception to the *Drop the E* rule.

Look for tricky parts.

Look at the words below.
Look for the tricky parts.
Use the six steps to help you
spell the words.

Remember to . . .

1. **Read the word slowly.**
2. **Mark any tricky part.**
3. **Study the tricky part.**
4. **Cover the word.**
5. **Write the word.**
6. **Check the spelling.**

true	_____
accept	_____
close	_____

chubby

There is a fish in England called *chub*.
The chub fish is thick and fat.
We get the word *chubby*
from the chubby chub fish.

Trying out your spelling tools

1— Your teacher will read a letter.
Listen. Finish the letter.

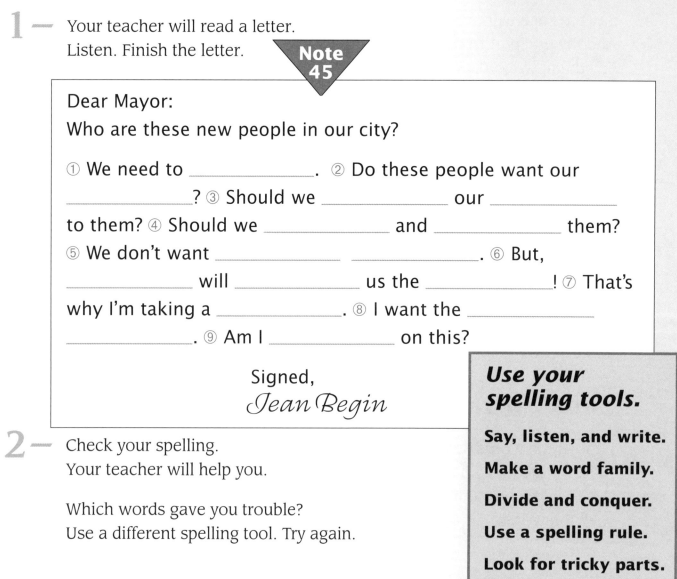

Note 45

Dear Mayor:
Who are these new people in our city?

① We need to _____. ② Do these people want our
_____? ③ Should we _____ our _____
to them? ④ Should we _____ and _____ them?
⑤ We don't want _____ _____. ⑥ But,
_____ will _____ us the _____! ⑦ That's
why I'm taking a _____. ⑧ I want the _____
_____. ⑨ Am I _____ on this?

Signed,
Jean Begin

2— Check your spelling.
Your teacher will help you.

Which words gave you trouble?
Use a different spelling tool. Try again.

Use your spelling tools.

Say, listen, and write.

Make a word family.

Divide and conquer.

Use a spelling rule.

Look for tricky parts.

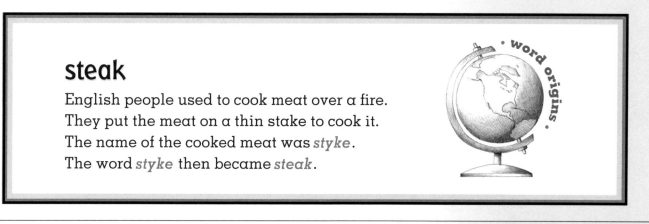

steak

English people used to cook meat over a fire.
They put the meat on a thin stake to cook it.
The name of the cooked meat was *styke*.
The word *styke* then became *steak*.

· word origins ·

3— Your teacher will read another letter.
You are going to spell new words.
This will give you a chance
to try out your spelling tools.

Note 46

Use your spelling tools.

Say, listen, and write.

Make a word family.

Divide and conquer.

Use a spelling rule.

Look for tricky parts.

Dear Jean Begin:
Regarding your letter to the mayor:

① A _____ _____ lives next
door. ② They're _____ Spain.
③ We _____ our arms to _____. ④ They
_____ us. ⑤ _____ they want to take
_____ jobs? ⑥ Should we _____ to rumours and
_____ ? ⑦ I _____ know. ⑧ I just know _____
friends.

Signed
A neighbour

4— Check your spelling.
Your teacher will help you.

Which words gave you trouble?
Use a different spelling tool.
Try again.

Applying your spelling tools

1— Look at this example.

Naomi thinks about
living in another country.

Here are her ideas.

Good things:
I would see new things.
It would be exciting.
It would be something different.
Hard things:
I would feel lonely.
It would be hard to get a good job.
I wouldn't know the language.

2— Your turn.

Would you like to live in a different country?

Why or why not?

I would like to live in another country because

(a) _____

(b) _____

(c) _____

I would not like to live in another country because

(a) _____

(b) _____

(c) _____

A final word

Which words about **community changes** would you like to add to your dictionary?

Practice words

began	posting	completed	dated	driver
permit	training	November	October	employed
ago	contract	presently	contact	number

Working with spelling tools

Say, listen, and write.

Say each word.
Listen to each sound.
Write the word as you say it.

posting _____	driver _____	November _____
ago _____	contact _____	permit _____
October _____	contract _____	number _____

If you say these words slowly,
you will have a good chance of spelling them right.

Make a word family.

Say this word: **train**

Think of words that rhyme.
Write the words.
Your teacher will help you
with the spelling.

Note 47

train

Look at your words.
Circle the words that belong
to the same word family as **train**.

Learn to spell one of these words, and
you will be able to spell
all of the words.

Divide and conquer.

How can you divide and conquer
these words?

ago

posting

training

employed

presently

began

Divide and conquer

Do you see
- ❏ **common beginning parts?**
- ❏ **common end parts?**
- ❏ **little words?**

Use a spelling rule.

Practice the *Silent E* rule.

Say the word.
Underline the long vowel sound.
Circle the silent **e**.

date	drive	complete

Silent E rule

When you add the letter *e*
to the end of a word,
the short vowel sound
in that word changes to
a long vowel sound.

Practice the *Drop the E* rule.

Say the base word.
Add the end part to the base word.
Say the new word.

Drop the E rule

If your word ends with
a *silent e*,
drop the *silent e*
before you add an end part
that starts with a vowel.

date + ed _____
date + ing _____
date + s _____
drive + er _____
drive + ing _____
drive + s _____
complete + s _____
complete + ed _____
complete + ing _____
complete + ly _____

· word origins ·

skating on thin ice

There used to be a sport called *tickledybendo*.
In this sport, the players had to skate on thin ice.
It was very dangerous. Sometimes, the ice broke.
Today, *skating on thin ice* means taking chances.

Look for tricky parts.

Look at the words below.
Look for the tricky parts.
Use the six steps to help you
spell the words.

employ _____

complete _____

Remember to . . .

1. **Read the word slowly.**
2. **Mark any tricky part.**
3. **Study the tricky part.**
4. **Cover the word.**
5. **Write the word.**
6. **Check the spelling.**

Trying out your spelling tools

1 — Your teacher will read a cover letter for a job.
Listen.
Finish the cover letter.

Note 48

① I saw your job _____ _____

_____ 1. ② It was asking for

a _____.

③ I _____ a course one year

_____. ④ I _____ my

_____ in _____. ⑤ I have

my _____. ⑥ I am _____

_____. ⑦ My _____ ends

this month.

⑧ Please _____ me at this _____.

Use your spelling tools.

Say, listen, and write.

Make a word family.

Divide and conquer.

Use a spelling rule.

Look for tricky parts.

2 — Check your spelling.
Your teacher will help you.

Which words gave you trouble?
Use a different spelling tool.
Try again.

3— Your teacher will read another cover leter.
You are going to spell new words.
This will give you a chance
to try out your spelling tools.

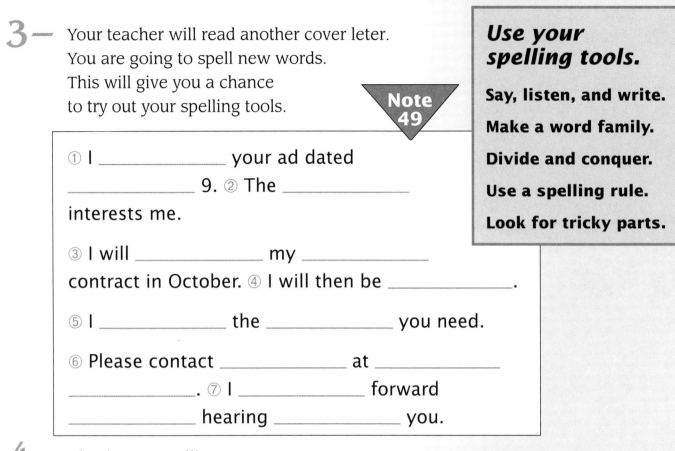

Note 49

Use your spelling tools.

Say, listen, and write.

Make a word family.

Divide and conquer.

Use a spelling rule.

Look for tricky parts.

① I _____ your ad dated
_____ 9. ② The _____
interests me.

③ I will _____ my _____
contract in October. ④ I will then be _____.

⑤ I _____ the _____ you need.

⑥ Please contact _____ at _____
_____. ⑦ I _____ forward
_____ hearing _____ you.

4— Check your spelling.
Your teacher will help you.

Which words gave you trouble?
Use a different spelling tool.
Try again.

Applying your spelling tools

1— Look at this example.

Sandy sees an
interesting ad for a job.

Here is Sandy's cover letter.

What is the job?

Dear Sir:

I saw your ad.

I love dogs. I have five of them.
I enjoy walking in the park.
I am sure your dogs will like me.

Please contact me at 211-3333.
I look forward to hearing from you.

Yours truly,
Sandy Boxer

Note 50

2 — Your turn.

You see these ads in the paper:
- Singer Wanted
- Dancer Wanted
- Cook Wanted
- Handyman Wanted
- Gardener Wanted

Write a cover letter for one of the jobs.

A final word

Which words about **work forms** would you like to add to your dictionary?

Practice words

punch	every	drag	hour	sometimes
quick	usually	hungry	fool	starving
hardly	myself	mostly	guys	breakfast

Working with spelling tools

Say, listen, and write.

Say each word.
Listen to each sound.
Write the word as you say it.

| punch _____ | starving _____ | most _____ |
| hard _____ | drag _____ | self _____ |

If you say these words slowly,
you will have a good chance
of spelling them right.

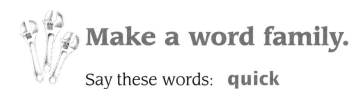

Make a word family.

Say these words: **quick**

Think of words that rhyme.
Write the words.
Your teacher will help you with the spelling.

Note
51

quick

Look at your words.
Circle the words that belong
to the same word family as **quick**.

Learn to spell one of these words, and
you will be able to spell
all of the words.

Say this word: **fool**

Think of words that rhyme.
Write the words.

Your teacher will help you with the spelling.

Note
52

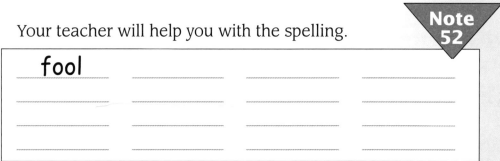

fool

Look at your words.
Circle the words that belong to the same word family as **fool**.

Learn to spell one of these words, and
you will be able to spell
all of the words.

✂ Divide and conquer.

How can you divide and conquer these words?

usually _____

mostly _____

sometimes _____

every _____

hardly _____

guys _____

myself _____

breakfast _____

Divide and conquer

Do you see
- ❑ common beginning parts?
- ❑ common end parts?
- ❑ little words?

Use a spelling rule.

Practice the *Doubling* rule.

Say the base word.
Add the end part to the base word.
Say the new word.

drag + ing _____

drag + ed _____

drag + s _____

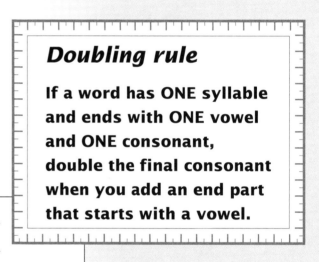

Doubling rule

If a word has ONE syllable and ends with ONE vowel and ONE consonant, double the final consonant when you add an end part that starts with a vowel.

mattress

The word *mattress* comes from the word *matrah*.
Matrah is an old Arab word.
It means *thick cushion*.
The word *matrah* became *materas* in English.
Years later, the word *materas* became *mattress*.

Practice the _Y_ rule (part 1).

Say the word.
Divide the word into syllables.
Underline the letter that
makes the long **e** sound.

every	_____
hungry	_____

Practice the _Y_ rule (part 2).

Say the base word.
Add the end part to the base word.
Say the new word.

hungry + er	_____
hungry + est	_____
hungry + ly	_____
guy + s	_____

The **Y** rule doesn't apply to
one of these words.
Which word is it?
Why doesn't the rule apply?

Practice the _Silent E_ rule.

Say the word.
Underline the long vowel sound.
Circle the silent **e**.

time

Y rule (part 1)

**When you hear
the _long e_ sound
at the end of a word
that has two syllables,
use _y_.**

**You have a good chance
of being right.**

Y rule (part 2)

**If a word ends in
consonant + y,
the _y_ changes to _i_
when you add all end parts
except _ing_.**

Silent E rule

**When you add the letter _e_
to the end of a word,
the short vowel sound
in that word changes to
a long vowel sound.**

Practice the *Drop the E* rule.

Say the base word.
Add the end part to the base word.
Say the new word.

time + ed	_____
time + ing	_____
time + s	_____
time + er	_____
time + ly	_____
starve + ed	_____
starve + s	_____
starve + ing	_____

Drop the E rule

**If your word ends with
a *silent e*,
drop the *silent e*
before you add an end part
that starts with a vowel.**

Look for tricky parts.

Look at the words below.
Look for the tricky parts.
Use the six steps to help you spell the word.

hour	_____
usual	_____
some	_____
every	_____
guy	_____
breakfast	_____

Remember to...

1. **Read the word slowly.**
2. **Mark any tricky part.**
3. **Study the tricky part.**
4. **Cover the word.**
5. **Write the word.**
6. **Check the spelling.**

moonshine

People used to make liquor sometimes.
Making liquor was against the law.
So, people made the liquor at night—under the light of the moon.
That's why they called the liquor *moonshine*.

word origins

Trying out your spelling tools

1— Your teacher will read a paragraph.
Listen.
Finish the ideas.

Note 53

I work in a shop.

① I _____ in _____ morning.

② _____, I eat a _____

_____. ③ But _____, I'm not

_____. ④ _____ I keep to _____.

⑤ I _____ talk to the other _____.

⑥ They're O.K. They _____ around a lot.

⑦ By lunch _____, I'm _____.

⑧ After lunch, the time can _____.

2— Check your spelling.
Your teacher will help you.

Which words gave you trouble?
Use a different spelling tool.
Try again.

3— Your teacher will read another paragraph.
You are going to spell new words.
This will give you a chance
to try out your spelling tools.

Use your spelling tools.

Say, listen, and write.

Make a word family.

Divide and conquer.

Use a spelling rule.

Look for tricky parts.

Note 54

① _____ jobs are _____ and
bad. ② _____ jobs are _____. ③ You need
a lot of _____. ④ But the _____ is
_____good. ⑤ _____ jobs are _____.
⑥ _____ the pay is lousy. ⑦ Or the job is
_____. ⑧ You _____ have _____.

4 — Check your spelling.
Your teacher will help you.

Which words gave you trouble?
Use a different spelling tool. Try again.

Applying your spelling tools

1 — Look at this example.

Tanya fills out a form
for her boss.

Do you think she is
telling the truth?

> Write *always*, *usually*, *sometimes*, or *never*
> after each question.
>
> 1. Are you ever late for work? _____ **never** _____
> 2. Do you ever leave early? _____ **never** _____
> 3. Do you say good things
>   about your boss? _____ **always**
> 4. Do you agree with your boss? _____ **always**
> 5. Do you ever hate your job? _____ **never**
> 6. Do you ever think your boss
>   is the best? _____ **always**

2 — Your turn.

Think about the best job you ever had.

Finish the ideas.

> **My Best Job Ever**
> 1. I always _____
> 2. I never_____
> 3. I sometimes _____
> 4. My boss usually _____
> 5. My boss hardly ever _____
> 6. Mostly, I liked _____

A final word

Which words about **work routines**
would you like to add to your dictionary?

unit
13

Practice words

thought	might	there's	cute	funny
what	said	heard	here's	giggle
finally	that's	strange	humdinger	groan

Working with spelling tools

Say, listen, and write.

Say each word.
Listen to each sound.
Write the word as you say it.

humdinger _____	that	_____

If you say these words slowly,
you will have a good chance
of spelling them right.

Make a word family.

Say this word: **might**

Think of words that rhyme.
Write the words.
Your teacher will help you with the spelling.

Note 55

might _____ _____
_____ _____ _____
_____ _____ _____
_____ _____ _____
_____ _____ _____

Look at your words.
Circle the words that belong to the same word family as **might**.

Learn to spell one of these words, and
you will be able to spell
all of the words.

Say this word: **thought**

Think of words that rhyme.
Write the words.
Your teacher will help you with the spelling.

Note 56

thought _____ _____
_____ _____ _____
_____ _____ _____
_____ _____ _____
_____ _____ _____

Look at your words.
Circle the words that belong to the same word family as **thought**.

Learn to spell one of these words, and
you will be able to spell all of the words.

Say this word: **giggle**

Think of words that rhyme.
Write the words.
Your teacher will help you with the spelling. ▽ **Note 57**

giggle _____ _____

_____ _____ _____

_____ _____ _____

Look at your words.
Circle the words that belong to the same word family as **giggle**.

Learn to spell one of these words, and
you will be able to spell
all of the words.

 ## Divide and conquer.

How can you divide and conquer
these words?

heard   _____
finally   _____
humdinger   _____
there's   _____
here's   _____
that's   _____
what   _____

Divide and conquer.

Do you see
❑ **common beginning parts?**
❑ **common end parts?**
❑ **little words?**

Use a spelling rule.

Practice the *Doubling* rule.

Say the base word.
Add the end part to the base word.
Say the new word.

fun + y	_____

> ## *Doubling rule*
>
> **If a word has ONE syllable and ends with ONE vowel and ONE consonant, double the final consonant when you add an end part that starts with a vowel.**

Practice the *Y* rule (part 1).

Say the word.
Divide the word into two syllables.
Underline the letter that makes the long **e** sound.

funny	_____

> ## *Y rule (part 1)*
>
> **When you hear the *long e* sound at the end of a word that has two syllables, use *y*.**
>
> **You have a good chance of being right.**

Practice the *Y* rule (part 2).

Say the base word.
Add the end part to the base word.
Say the new word.

funny + er	_____
funny + est	_____

> ## *Y rule (part 2)*
>
> **If a word ends in *consonant + y*, the *y* changes to *i* when you add all end parts except *ing*.**

Practice the *Silent E* rule.

Say the word.
Underline the long vowel sound.
Circle the silent **e**.

here	cute	strange

> ## *Silent E rule*
>
> **When you add the letter *e* to the end of a word, the short vowel sound in that word changes to a long vowel sound.**

Practice the *Drop the E* rule.

Say the base word.
Add the end part to the base word.
Say the new word.

giggle + ed _____

giggle + ing _____

giggle + s _____

giggle + er _____

giggle + y _____

strange + er _____

strange + est _____

strange + ly _____

cute + er _____

cute + est _____

cute + ly _____

Drop the E rule

If your word ends with
a *silent e*,
drop the *silent e*
before you add an end part
that starts with a vowel.

Look for tricky parts.

Look at the words below.
Look for the tricky parts.
Use the six steps to help you
spell the words.

final _____

there _____

heard _____

groan _____

what _____

Remember to...

1. Read the word slowly.

2. Mark any tricky part.

3. Study the tricky part.

4. Cover the word.

5. Write the word.

6. Check the spelling.

Trying out your spelling tools

1— Your teacher will read some sentences.
Listen. Finish the sentences.

Note 58

① _____ this _____ give
you a _____ .
② _____ this _____ the
other day.
③ This will make you _____ .
④ Too _____ , eh?
⑤ Too _____ , eh?
⑥ _____ a good one.
⑦ _____ this guy . . .
⑧ She _____ , " _____ ?"
⑨ He _____ says . . .
⑩ _____ a _____ one, eh?

Use your spelling tools.

Say, listen, and write.

Make a word family.

Divide and conquer.

Use a spelling rule.

Look for tricky parts.

2— Check your spelling.
Your teacher will help you.

Which words gave you trouble?
Use a different spelling tool.
Try again.

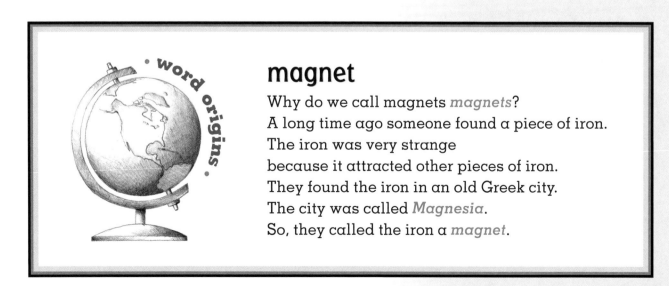

word origins

magnet

Why do we call magnets *magnets*?
A long time ago someone found a piece of iron.
The iron was very strange
because it attracted other pieces of iron.
They found the iron in an old Greek city.
The city was called *Magnesia*.
So, they called the iron a *magnet*.

3— Your teacher will read some more sentences.
You are going to spell new words.
This will give you a chance
to try out your spelling tools.

▼ **Note 59**

Use your spelling tools.

Say, listen, and write.

Make a word family.

Divide and conquer.

Use a spelling rule.

Look for tricky parts.

① Here's a _____ one.

② Here are a few _____ for you.

③ These are the _____
_____!

④ Here's a _____.

⑤ _____ a _____ for sore eyes!

⑥ _____ has got to be the _____!

⑦_____ _____ my favourite _____.

⑧ I've _____ _____ now!

4— Check your spelling.
Your teacher will help you.

Which words gave you trouble?
Use a different spelling tool.
Try again.

Applying your spelling tools

1— Look at this example.

Someone put this
on the memo board at work.

If life hands you a lemon,
squeeze it
and make lemonade.

Thought you guys would like this one.

2— Your turn.

Do you have a favourite saying or joke?

Write it here.
Post it on the memo board.

A final word

Which words about **memo board**
would you like to add
to your dictionary?

unit 14

work Relations

Practice words

along	fire	whine	maybe	advice
quite	awful	bad	mistake	complain
gripe	argue	respect	hide	office

Working with spelling tools

Say, listen, and write.

Say each word.
Listen to each sound.
Write the word as you say it.

along _____	bad _____	respect _____

If you say these words slowly,
you will have a good chance
of spelling them right.

Divide and conquer.

How can you divide and conquer these words?

along ———————————————

maybe ———————————————

complain ———————————————

advice ———————————————

mistake ———————————————

office ———————————————

Divide and conquer

Do you see
- ❐ common beginning parts?
- ❐ common end parts?
- ❐ little words?

Use a spelling rule.

Practice the *Doubling* rule.

Say the base word.
Add the end part to the base word.
Say the new word.

bad + ly   ———————————————

Doubling rule

If a word has ONE syllable and ends with ONE vowel and ONE consonant, double the final consonant when you add an end part that starts with a vowel.

Practice the *Silent E* rule.

Say the base word.
Underline the long vowel sound.
Circle the silent **e**.

fire	advice	gripe
hide	whine	mistake
	quite	

Silent E rule

When you add the letter *e* to the end of a word, the short vowel sound in that word changes to a long vowel sound.

Practice the *Drop the E* rule.

Say the base word.
Add the end part to the base word.
Say the new word.

fire + ed	_____
fire + ing	_____
fire + s	_____
whine + er	_____
whine + ing	_____
whine + ed	_____
whine + s	_____
mistake + s	_____
gripe + ing	_____
gripe + s	_____
gripe + er	_____
gripe + ed	_____
hide + ing	_____
hide + s	_____
argue + s	_____
argue + ed	_____
argue + ing	_____
office + s	_____

Drop the E rule

**If your word ends with
a *silent e*,
drop the *silent e*
before you add an end part
that starts with a vowel.**

word origins

bimbo

Bimbo is the Italian word for *baby*.
Years ago, unimportant men
were called *bimbos*.
Now, only women are sometimes called *bimbos*.

Look for tricky parts.

Look at the words below.
Look for the tricky parts.
Use the six steps to help you
spell the words.

awful _____
complain _____
whine _____
argue _____

Remember to...

1. **Read the word slowly.**
2. **Mark any tricky part.**
3. **Study the tricky part.**
4. **Cover the word.**
5. **Write the word.**
6. **Check the spelling.**

Trying out your spelling rules

1 — Your teacher will read a letter.
Listen.
Finish the letter.

Note 60

Use your spelling tools.

Say, listen, and write.

Make a word family.

Divide and conquer.

Use a spelling rule.

Look for tricky parts.

Help me Beatrice!
① This job was a _____
_____ . ② All we do is _____
and _____ . ③ The bosses
_____ in their _____ .
④ They_____ and _____ .
⑤ There's no _____ . ⑥ It's _____
_____ . ⑦ Nobody gets _____ .
⑧ _____ they'll _____ me.
⑨ Any _____ ?
Miss you awfully,
Spike

2 — Check your spelling. Your teacher will help you.

Which words gave you trouble?
Use a different spelling tool. Try again.

3— Your teacher will read another letter.
You are going to spell new words.
This will give you a chance
to try out your spelling tools.

Note 61

Hi Spike,

① The job sounds _____ bad. ② And _____ bosses _____ worse! ③ _____ in their _____. ④ _____ and _____.

⑤ What's _____ with _____?

⑥ Hang in _____ _____ Christmas.

⑦ Then maybe you _____ quit.

Beatrice

4— Check your spelling.
Your teacher will help you.

Which words gave you trouble?
Use a different spelling tool.
Try again.

Use your spelling tools.

Say, listen, and write.

Make a word family.

Divide and conquer.

Use a spelling rule.

Look for tricky parts.

Applying your spelling tools

1— Look at this example.

Alice fills out
a survey
about her job.

Does Alice like
her job?

Work Relations

Answer these questions.
Write **yes, no** or **not really**.

1. Do you get along with people at work? ___not really___
2. Do you gripe a lot? _____ yes
3. Do you respect your boss?_____ not really
4. Does your boss respect you?_____ not really
5. Does your boss help you when you need it? __no__

$2-$ Your turn.

Think about work and people.

Finish these ideas.

At work, people should

1. _____

2. _____

At work, people shouldn't

1. _____

2. _____

A final word

Which words about **work relations**
would you like to add
to your dictionary?

knock on wood

Do you ever *knock on wood*
to stop something bad from happening?
People did the same thing a long time ago.
People used to believe
that spirits lived in trees.
They rapped on the trees
to ask the spirits to protect them.
Now, we don't rap on trees and talk to spirits.
We just *knock on wood*.

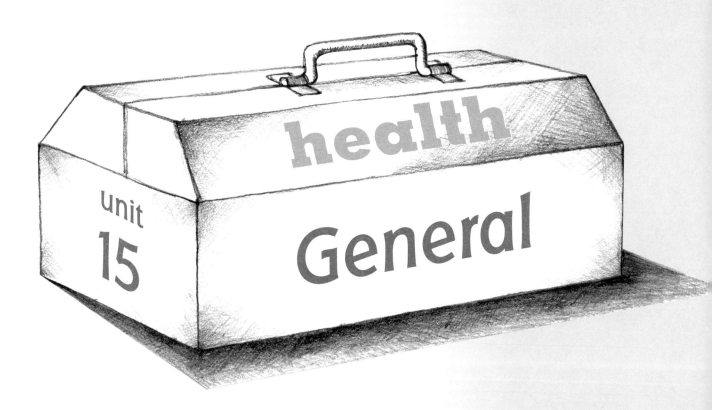

Practice words

broken	doctor	accident	stiff	blue
hospital	x-rays	ankle	sprained	cast
strained	crutches	sling	hurt	black

Working with spelling tools

Say, listen, and write.

Say each word.
Listen to each sound.
Write the word as you say it.

cast _____	sling _____

If you say these words slowly,
you will have a good chance
of spelling them right.

Make a word family.

Say these words: **strain   sprain**

Think of words that rhyme.
Write the words.
Your teacher will help you with the spelling.

Note 62

strain
sprain

Look at your words.
Circle the words that belong
to the same word family as **strain** and **sprain**.

Learn to spell one of these words, and
you will be able to spell all of the words.

Say this word: **black**

Think of words that rhyme.
Write the words.
Your teacher will help you with the spelling.

Note 63

black

Look at your words.
Circle the words that belong
to the same word family as **black**.

Learn to spell one of these words, and
you will be able to spell all of the words.

Say this word: **crutch**

Think of words that rhyme.
Write the words.
Your teacher will help you with the spelling.

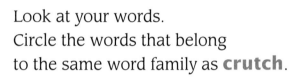

Note 64

crutch _____ _____

_____ _____ _____

_____ _____ _____

Look at your words.
Circle the words that belong
to the same word family as **crutch**.

Learn to spell one of these words, and
you will be able to spell
all of the words.

Divide and conquer.

How can you divide and conquer
these words?

x-rays _____

broken _____

doctor _____

strained _____

crutches _____

sprained _____

accident _____

Divide and conquer

Do you see
❒ **common beginning parts?**
❒ **common end parts?**
❒ **little words?**

Trying out your spelling tools

1— Your teacher will read a letter.
You are going to spell new words.
This will give you a chance
to try out your spelling tools.

Note 65

Suzy!
What happened?

① _____, _____ and crutches! Oh my! ② How's _____ _____? ③ How's _____ ankle?

④ Your dad _____ _____ finger.
⑤ _____ put a _____ on it. ⑥ You _____ how he hates _____ and _____. ⑦ He _____ want to go.

⑧ _____! When it _____, it pours. ⑨ Keep me _____ on what's _____.

Mom

2— Check your spelling.
Your teacher will help you.

Use your spelling tools.

Say, listen, and write.

Make a word family.

Divide and conquer.

Use a spelling rule.

Look for tricky parts.

· word origins ·

fancy footwork

The term *fancy footwork* comes from boxing.
Boxers have to move their feet well.
People used to say that a good boxer
used a lot of fancy footwork.
Today we use *fancy footwork*
to get out of a bad situation.

Applying your spelling tools

1— Look at this example.

Jerry's daughter was in an accident.

Jerry writes a note to the teacher.

Dear Miss Chase,

My daughter was in a car accident.
She's in the hospital.
She broke her leg.
The doctor says she's O.K.
She'll be back at school next week.

Yours truly,
Jerry Days

2— Your turn.

Someone you know got hurt.

Write a note to tell somebody about it.

A final word

Which words about **general health** would you like to add to your dictionary?

Practice words

tsp.	dice	oven	chop	canned
frozen	boil	sprinkle	garnish	chilled
bowl	stove	serve	tbsp	taste

Working with spelling tools

Say, listen, and write.

Say each word.
Listen to each sound.
Write the word as you say it.

chop _____   frozen _____   garnish _____

If you say these words slowly,
you will have a good chance
of spelling them right.

Make a word family.

Say this word: **boil**

Think of words that rhyme.
Write the words.
Your teacher will help you with the spelling.

Note
66

boil _____ _____

_____ _____ _____

_____ _____ _____

Look at your words.
Circle the words that belong
to the same word family as **boil**.

Learn to spell one of these words, and
you will be able to spell
all of the words.

Say this word: **sprinkle**

Think of words that rhyme.
Write the words.
Your teacher will help you with the spelling.

Note
67

sprinkle _____ _____

_____ _____ _____

_____ _____ _____

Look at your words.
Circle the words that belong
to the same word family as **sprinkle**.

Learn to spell one of these words, and
you will be able to spell
all of the words.

Say this word: **dice**

Think of words that rhyme.
Write the words.
Your teacher will help you with the spelling.   **Note 68**

dice _____ _____
_____ _____ _____

Look at your words.
Circle the words that belong
to the same word family as **dice**.

Learn to spell one of these words, and
you will be able to spell
all of the words.

✂ Divide and conquer.

How can you divide and conquer
this word?

chilled _____

Divide and conquer

Do you see
❏ **common beginning parts?**
❏ **common end parts?**
❏ **little words?**

word origins

paper
A long time ago, paper was made from a plant.
The plant grew in Egypt.
The plant was called *papyrus*.
The papyrus was soaked in water.
Then the papyrus was pressed into sheets.
The word *papyrus* became *papier* in French.
Then, the word *papier* became *paper* in English.

Use a spelling rule.

Practice the *Doubling* rule.

Say the base word.
Add the end part to the base word.
Say the new word.

chop + ing	_____
chop + ed	_____
chop + s	_____
chop + er	_____
can + s	_____
can + ed	_____
can + ing	_____

Doubling rule

If a word has ONE syllable and ends with ONE vowel and ONE consonant, double the final consonant when you add an end part that starts with a vowel.

Practice the *Silent E* rule.

Say the word.
Underline
the long vowel sound.
Circle the silent **e.**

dice	froze
stove	taste

Silent E rule

When you add the letter *e* to the end of a word, the short vowel sound in that word changes to a long vowel sound.

humdrum

Bees make a humming sound.
The humming sound never changes.
The word *hum* sounds like *drum*.
People put *hum* and *drum* together.
Now *humdrum* means *boring*—never changing.

Practice the *Drop the E* rule.

Say the base word.
Add the end part to the base word.
Say the new word.

dice + ed _____

dice + ing _____

dice + s _____

dice + er _____

dice + y _____

stove + s _____

taste + s _____

taste + ed _____

taste + ing _____

taste + s _____

taste + y _____

taste + er _____

froze + en _____

serve + s _____

serve + ed _____

serve + ing _____

serve + er _____

sprinkle + s _____

sprinkle + ing _____

sprinkle + er _____

sprinkle + ed _____

Look for tricky parts.

Look at the words below.
Look for the tricky parts.
Use the six steps to help you
spell the words.

tsp.   _____

chill   _____

serve   _____

bowl   _____

tbsp.   _____

oven   _____

Remember to...

1. Read the word slowly.

2. Mark any tricky part.

3. Study the tricky part.

4. Cover the word.

5. Write the word.

6. Check the spelling.

Trying out your spelling tools

1 — Your teacher will read some directions.
Listen. Finish the sentences.

Note 69

① Heat _____ to 350°F.

② _____ water on _____.

③ Add 2 _____ pepper and salt.

④ _____ and _____ fruit.

⑤ Add _____ peas to _____.

⑥ Mix in _____ corn.

⑦ Add 1 _____ butter.

⑧ _____ with sugar to _____.

⑨ _____ with mint.

⑩ _____ with _____ drinks.

Use your spelling tools.

Say, listen, and write.

Make a word family.

Divide and conquer.

Use a spelling rule.

Look for tricky parts.

2 — Check your spelling.
Your teacher will help you.

Which words gave you trouble?
Use a different spelling tool. Try again.

3 — Your teacher will read a recipe.
You are going to spell new words.
This will give you a chance
to try out your spelling tools.

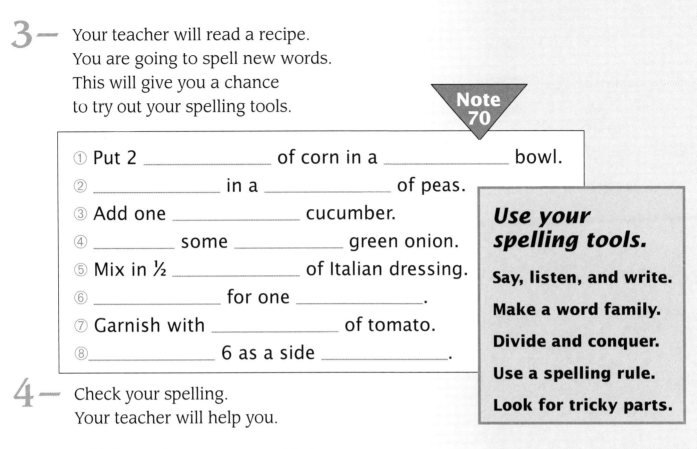

▼ **Note 70**

① Put 2 _____ of corn in a _____ bowl.

② _____ in a _____ of peas.

③ Add one _____ cucumber.

④ _____ some _____ green onion.

⑤ Mix in ½ _____ of Italian dressing.

⑥ _____ for one _____.

⑦ Garnish with _____ of tomato.

⑧ _____ 6 as a side _____.

Use your spelling tools.

Say, listen, and write.

Make a word family.

Divide and conquer.

Use a spelling rule.

Look for tricky parts.

4 — Check your spelling.
Your teacher will help you.

Which words gave you trouble?
Use a different spelling tool.
Try again.

Applying your spelling tools

1 — Look at this example.

Here is Perry's
favourite recipe.

Would you eat this?

Grilled Fish

Put fish on tin foil.
Sprinkle with icing sugar.
Add 1 cup ketchup.
Crinkle ends of tin foil around fish.
Grill until flaky.

2— Your turn.

What is your favourite recipe?

Write it here.

A final word

Which words about *diet* would you like to add to your dictionary?

Practice words

weigh	gain	weight	lazy	exercise
gym	should	stretch	tone	flab
lift	tennis	playing	laps	begin

Working with spelling tools

Say, listen, and write.

Say each word.
Listen to each sound.
Write the word as you say it.

flab _____   lift _____
laps _____   begin _____

If you say these words slowly,
you will have a good chance
of spelling them right.

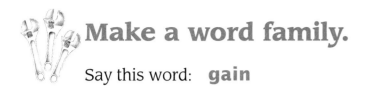

Make a word family.

Say this word: **gain**

Think of words that rhyme.
Write the words.
Your teacher will help you with the spelling.

Note 71

gain

Look at your words.
Circle the words that belong
to the same word family as **gain**.

Learn to spell one of these words, and
you will be able to spell
all of the words.

Say this word: **should**

Think of words that rhyme.
Write the words.
Your teacher will help you with the spelling.

Note 72

should

Look at your words.
Circle the words that belong
to the same word family as **should**.

Learn to spell one of these words, and
you will be able to spell
all of the words.

Say this word: **stretch**

Think of words that rhyme.
Write the words.
Your teacher will help you with the spelling.

Note 73

stretch _____ _____

_____ _____ _____

_____ _____ _____

Look at your words.
Circle the words that belong
to the same word family as **stretch**.

Learn to spell one of these words, and you will be able to spell
all of the words.

Divide and conquer.

How can you divide and conquer
these words?

playing _____
laps _____
tennis _____
begin _____

> ### Divide and conquer
>
> **Do you see**
> ❐ **common beginning parts?**
> ❐ **common end parts?**
> ❐ **little words?**

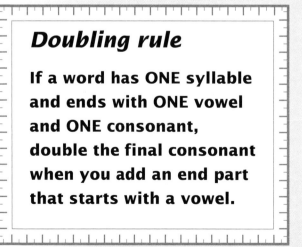

Use a spelling rule.

Practice the *Doubling* rule.

Say the base word.
Add the end part to the base word.
Say the new word.

flab + y _____

> ### Doubling rule
>
> If a word has ONE syllable
> and ends with ONE vowel
> and ONE consonant,
> double the final consonant
> when you add an end part
> that starts with a vowel.

Practice the *Y* rule (part 1).

Say the word.
Divide the word into two syllables.
Underline the letter that makes
the long **e** sound.

lazy	_____
flabby	_____

Practice the *Y* rule (part 2).

Say the base word.
Add the end part to the base word.
Say the new word.

lazy	+	er	_____
lazy	+	est	_____
lazy	+	ly	_____
flabby	+	er	_____
flabby	+	est	_____
play	+	s	_____
play	+	ing	_____
play	+	ed	_____
play	+	er	_____

The **Y** rule does not apply to some of these words.
Which ones? Why?

Practice the *Silent E* rule.

Say the word.
Underline the long vowel sound.
Circle the silent **e**.

tone	exercise

Y rule (part 1)

When you hear
the *long e* sound
at the end of a word
that has two syllables,
use *y*.

You have a good chance
of being right.

Y rule (part 2)

If a word ends in
consonant + y,
the *y* changes to *i*
when you add all end parts
except *ing*.

Silent E rule

When you add the letter *e*
to the end of a word,
the short vowel sound
in that word changes to
a long vowel sound.

Practice the *Drop the E* rule.

Say the base word.
Add the end part to the base word.
Say the new word.

tone + ed _____

tone + ing _____

tone + s _____

tone + er _____

exercise + ing _____

exercise + ed _____

exercise + s _____

exercise + er _____

Look for tricky parts.

Look at the words below.
Look for the tricky parts.
Use the six steps to help you
spell the words.

Remember to...

1. **Read the word slowly.**
2. **Mark any tricky part.**
3. **Study the tricky part.**
4. **Cover the word.**
5. **Write the word.**
6. **Check the spelling.**

weigh _____

weight _____

gym _____

play _____

exercise _____

word origins

candy

Greek soldiers used to eat a sweet food.
The food was covered in honey.
The food was called *kand*.
Kand became *candy* in English.

Trying out your spelling rules

1— Your teacher will read a paragraph.
Listen. Finish the ideas.

Note
74

① I'm so _____. ② I _____ _____ more.
③ I need to _____ and _____. ④ I'm all
_____. ⑤ I don't want to _____ _____.
⑥ I'm afraid to _____ myself. ⑦ I'll start _____
_____. ⑧ I'll _____ weights. ⑨ I'll run
_____. I'll join a _____. ⑩ I'll _____
tomorrow.

2— Check your spelling.
Your teacher will help you.

Which words gave you trouble?
Use a different spelling tool. Try again.

3— Your teacher will read
another paragraph.

You are going to spell new words.
This will give you a chance
to try out your spelling tools.

Use your spelling tools.

Say, listen, and write.

Make a word family.

Divide and conquer.

Use a spelling rule.

Look for tricky parts.

Note
75

① _____ _____ come and
gone. ② So much for _____. ③ Good-bye _____
and _____. ④ Hello _____ body.
⑤ I _____ exercise _____. ⑥ I just _____
have the time. ⑦ _____ buy some _____ at
Christmas. ⑧ I'll _____ _____ in the new year.
⑨ Come _____ _____ _____!

4— Check your spelling. Your teacher will help you.

Which words gave you trouble?
Use a different spelling tool. Try again.

Applying your spelling tools

1— Look at this example.

Gretchen gets
this form
in the mail.

She fills it out
for a free visit
to Gym Land.

> **ONE TIME OFFER**
> One free visit to Gym Land
> Just fill in this form.
>
> (a) What kind of fitness class would you like to do?
> ☐ toning ☐ stretching ☐ aerobic exercise ☑ weights
>
> (b) What do you want to focus on?
> ☐ weight ☐ ·exibility ☐ cardio ☑ strength
>
> (c) What do you presently do for exercise?
> *walk*
> *bowling*

2— Your turn.

You get this form
in the mail.

Fill it out
for a free visit
to Gym Land.

> **ONE TIME OFFER**
> One free visit to Gym Land
> Just fill in this form.
>
> (a) What kind of fitness class would you like to do?
> ☐ toning ☐ stretching ☐ aerobic exercise ☐ weights
>
> (b) What do you want to focus on?
> ☐ weight ☐ ·exibility ☐ cardio ☐ strength
>
> (c) What do you presently do for exercise?
> _____
> _____
> _____

A final word

Which words about **fitness**
would you like to add to your dictionary?

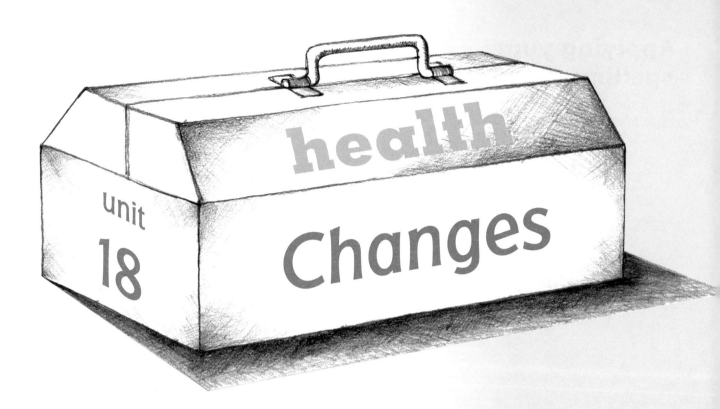

Practice words

news	changes	really	father	died
ill	age	death	shock	believe
gone	son-in-law	expecting	born	heart

Working with spelling tools

Say, listen, and write.

Say each word.
Listen to each sound.
Write the word as you say it.

expecting _____	born _____

If you say these words slowly,
you will have a good chance
of spelling them right.

Make a word family.

Say this word: **ill**

Think of words that rhyme.
Write the words.
Your teacher will help you with the spelling.

Note
76

ill _____   _____   _____   _____

_____   _____   _____   _____

_____   _____   _____   _____

_____   _____   _____   _____

Look at your words.
Circle the words that belong
to the same word family as **ill**.

Learn to spell one of these words, and
you will be able to spell
all of the words.

Say this word: **shock**

Think of words that rhyme.
Write the words.
Your teacher will help you with the spelling.

Note
77

shock _____   _____   _____   _____

_____   _____   _____   _____

_____   _____   _____   _____

_____   _____   _____   _____

Look at your words.
Circle the words that belong
to the same word family as **shock**.

Learn to spell one of these words, and
you will be able to spell
all of the words.

Divide and conquer.

How can you divide and conquer these words?

news _____
expecting _____
believe _____
changes _____
really _____
son-in-law _____
heart _____
father _____

Divide and conquer

Do you see
- ❏ common beginning parts?
- ❏ common end parts?
- ❏ little words?

Use a spelling rule.

Practice the *Silent E* rule.

Say the word.
Underline the long vowel sound.
Circle the silent **e**.

age   change

Silent E rule

When you add the letter *e* to the end of a word, the short vowel sound in that word changes to a long vowel sound.

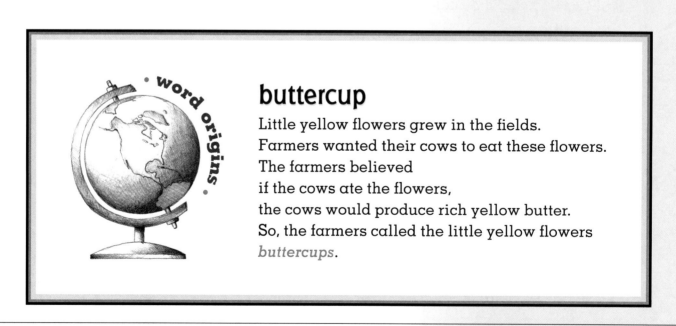

word origins

buttercup

Little yellow flowers grew in the fields.
Farmers wanted their cows to eat these flowers.
The farmers believed
if the cows ate the flowers,
the cows would produce rich yellow butter.
So, the farmers called the little yellow flowers
buttercups.

Practice the *Drop the E* rule.

Say the base word.
Add the end part to the base word.
Say the new word.

age + ed	_____
age + ing	_____
age + s	_____
change + s	_____
change + ing	_____
change + ed	_____
believe + s	_____
believe + ed	_____
believe + ing	_____
believe + er	_____
die + ed	_____
die + s	_____
die + ing*	_____

*Dying is an exception to the *Drop the E* rule.

Look for tricky parts.

Look at the words below.
Look for the tricky parts.
Use the six steps to help you spell the words.

news	_____
believe	_____
died	_____
death	_____
gone	_____
really	_____
son-in-law	_____

Remember to...

1. **Read the word slowly.**
2. **Mark any tricky part.**
3. **Study the tricky part.**
4. **Cover the word.**
5. **Write the word.**
6. **Check the spelling.**

Trying out your spelling tools

1 — Your teacher will read a letter.
Listen.
Finish the letter.

Note 78

Merry Christmas, Lucy!

① *There is lots of _____.* ② *There have been many*
_____. ③ *My _____ _____. It was*
his_____. ④ *He was _____ _____.*
⑤ *Still, his _____ was a _____.* ⑥ *He lived to*
a good old _____. ⑦ *But I can't _____ he's*
_____.

⑧ *I have a new _____.* ⑨ *My daughter is*
_____. ⑩ *The baby will be _____ in July.*

Take care,
Helga

2 — Check your spelling.
Your teacher will help you.

Which words gave you trouble?
Use a different spelling tool.
Try again.

> **Use your spelling tools.**
>
> **Say, listen, and write.**
>
> **Make a word family.**
>
> **Divide and conquer.**
>
> **Use a spelling rule.**
>
> **Look for tricky parts.**

word origins

broom

British women used to clean the floors
with a handful of twigs.
The twigs came from a shrub.
The shrub was called *broom*.

3— Your teacher will read another letter.
You are going to spell new words.
This will give you a chance
to try out your spelling tools.

Note 79

Use your spelling tools.

Say, listen, and write.

Make a word family.

Divide and conquer.

Use a spelling rule.

Look for tricky parts.

Hi, Helga. Merry Christmas!

① So sorry to hear _____ your dad.

② Life _____ brings _____.

③ _____ dad _____ a good man.

④ I'm _____ in London. ⑤ I _____ to be here for _____. ⑥ My _____ lives _____ now, too. ⑦ It's _____ nice having her here. ⑧ Other than that, _____ _____.

Send pictures of the baby next year.

Lucy

4— Check your spelling.
Your teacher will help you.

Which words gave you trouble?
Use a different spelling tool.
Try again.

Applying your spelling tools

1— Look at this example.

Dell sends
a Christmas note.

Hi guys,

Merry Christmas.
Another year has gone by.
Big news!
We have a son.
It's really great to be parents!

Hope all is well with you.

Dell & Angela

2— Your turn.

Send a Christmas note
to a friend.

Talk about changes
in the past year.

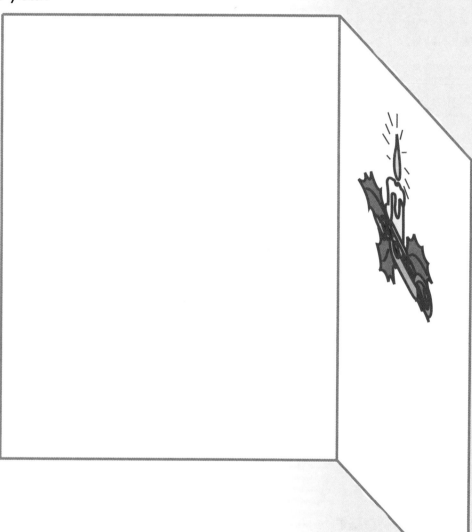

A final word

Which words about **changes**
would you like to add
to your dictionary?

Practice words

wax	bills	soap	bring	glasses
roll	sort	toilet	foil	Thursday
ask	coat	invite	drop	toothpaste

Working with spelling tools

Say, listen, and write.

Say each word.
Listen to each sound.
Write the word as you say it.

wax	_____	bring	_____	sort	_____
ask	_____	drop	_____		

If you say these words slowly,
you will have a good chance
of spelling them right.

Make a word family.

Say this word: **foil**

Think of words that rhyme.
Write the words.
Your teacher will help you with the spelling.

foil

Look at your words.
Circle the words that belong
to the same word family as **foil**.

Learn to spell one of these words, and
you will be able to spell
all of the words.

Say this word: **glass**

Think of words that rhyme.
Write the words.
Your teacher will help you with the spelling.

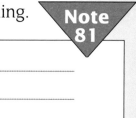

glass

Look at your words.
Circle the words that belong
to the same word family as **glass**.

Learn to spell one of these words, and
you will be able to spell
all of the words.

Say this word: **coat**

Think of words that rhyme.
Write the words.
Your teacher will help you with the spelling.

Note 82

coat _____   _____   _____

_____   _____   _____

_____   _____   _____

_____   _____   _____

_____

Look at your words.
Circle the words that belong
to the same word family as **coat**.

Learn to spell one of these words, and
you will be able to spell all of the words.

Say this word: **bill**

Think of words that rhyme.
Write the words.
Your teacher will help you with the spelling.

Note 83

bill _____   _____   _____

_____   _____   _____

_____   _____   _____

_____   _____   _____

_____

Look at your words.
Circle the words that belong
to the same word family as **bill**.

Learn to spell one of these words, and
you will be able to spell all of the words.

Divide and conquer.

How can you divide and conquer these words?

bills	_____
invite	_____
toothpaste	_____
glasses	_____
Thursday	_____
toilet	_____

Divide and conquer

Do you see
- ❑ **common beginning parts?**
- ❑ **common end parts?**
- ❑ **little words?**

Use a spelling rule.

Practice the *Doubling* rule.

Say the base word.
Add the end part to the base word.
Say the new word.

drop + ing	_____
drop + ed	_____
drop + s	_____
drop + er	_____
wax*+ ed	_____
wax + ing	_____
wax + s	_____

Doubling rule

**If a word has ONE syllable
and ends with ONE vowel
and ONE consonant,
double the final consonant
when you add an end part
that starts with a vowel.**

*Do not use the *Doubling* rule with the letter **x**.
You never see **xx** in English spelling.

Practice the *Silent E* rule.

Say the word.
Underline the long vowel sound.
Circle the silent **e**.

invite   paste

Silent E rule

**When you add the letter *e*
to the end of a word,
the short vowel sound
in that word changes to
a long vowel sound.**

Practice the *Drop the E* rule.

Say the base word.
Add the end part to the base word.
Say the new word.

invite + ed _____

invite + ing _____

invite + s _____

paste + ed _____

paste + ing _____

paste + y _____

paste + s _____

Look for tricky parts.

Look at the words below.
Look for the tricky parts.
Use the six steps to help you
spell the words.

tooth _____

toilet _____

soap _____

roll _____

Thursday _____

shampoo

The word *shampoo* comes from *champo*.
Champo is a Hindi word.
Champo means *massage*.

Trying out your spelling tools

1— Your teacher will read a to-do list.
Listen. Finish the list.

Note 84

① Get _____, _____ paper,

one _____ _____ paper,

_____ wrap, hand _____.

② _____ in _____.

③ _____ out _____.

④ _____ Suni about work stuff.

⑤ _____ Leo for_____.

⑥ _____ off Mom's _____.

2— Check your spelling.
Your teacher will help you.

Which words gave you trouble?
Use a different spelling tool. Try again.

3— Your teacher will read another to-do list.
You are going to spell new words.
This will give you a chance
to try out your spelling tools.

Note 85

Use your spelling tools.

Say, listen, and write.

Make a word family.

Divide and conquer.

Use a spelling rule.

Look for tricky parts.

I've already...

① _____ _____ Mom's coat

② _____ out bills

③ _____ Leo for Thursday

④ _____ Suni _____ work

I still have to...

⑤ _____ _____ to work

⑥ _____ _____ glasses

⑦ pick up _____ _____ _____ mom

⑧ _____ water _____

$4-$ Check your spelling.
Your teacher will help you.

Which words gave you trouble?
Use a different spelling tool.
Try again.

Applying your spelling tools

$1-$ Look at this example.

Here is Cleo's to-do list.

What is Cleo's job?

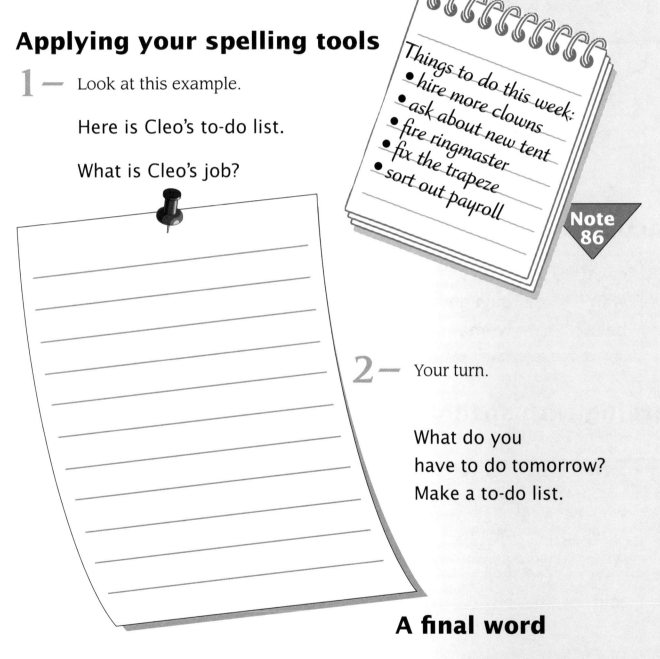

Things to do this week:
- hire more clowns
- ask about new tent
- fire ringmaster
- fix the trapeze
- sort out payroll

Note 86

$2-$ Your turn.

What do you
have to do tomorrow?
Make a to-do list.

A final word

Which words about **to-do lists**
would you like to add
to your dictionary?

Practice words

can't	guess	another	sure	doesn't
wait	daylight	honestly	shame	only
been	woman	they're	told	path

Working with spelling tools

Say, listen, and write.

Say each word.
Listen to each sound.
Write the word as you say it.

told _____   path _____

If you say these words slowly,
you will have a good chance
of spelling them right.

Make a word family.

Say this word: **other**

Think of words that rhyme.
Write the words.
Your teacher will help you with the spelling.

Note 87

__other__ _____ _____

_____ _____ _____

_____ _____ _____

Look at your words.
Circle the words that belong
to the same word family as **other**.

Learn to spell one of these words, and
you will be able to spell
all of the words.

Say this word: **light**

Think of words that rhyme.
Write the words.
Your teacher will help you with the spelling.

Note 88

__light__ _____ _____

_____ _____ _____

_____ _____ _____

_____ _____ _____

_____ _____ _____

Look at your words.
Circle the words that belong
to the same word family as **light**.

Learn to spell one of these words, and
you will be able to spell
all of the words.

Divide and conquer.

How can you divide and conquer
these words?

can't _____

daylight _____

they're _____

doesn't _____

honestly _____

only _____

another _____

woman _____

Divide and conquer

Do you see
- ☐ **common beginning parts?**
- ☐ **common end parts?**
- ☐ **little words?**

Use a spelling rule.

Practice the *Y* rule (part 1).

Say the word.
Divide the word into two syllables.
Underline the letter that makes
the long **e** sound.

only _____

Y rule (part 1)

**When you hear
the *long e* sound
at the end of a word
that has two syllables,
use *y*.**

**You have a good chance
of being right.**

Practice the *Silent E* rule.

Say the word.
Underline the long
vowel sound.
Circle the silent **e**.

sure   shame

Silent E rule

**When you add the letter *e*
to the end of a word,
the short vowel sound in that word
changes to a long vowel sound.**

Practice the *Drop the E* rule.

Say the base word.
Add the end part to the base word.
Say the new word.

sure + ly	_____
sure + est	_____
shame + s	_____
shame + ed	_____
shame + ing	_____

Look for tricky parts.

Look at the words below.
Look for the tricky parts.
Use the six steps to help you
spell the words.

sure	_____
day	_____
only	_____
wait	_____
woman	_____
does	_____
honest	_____
been	_____

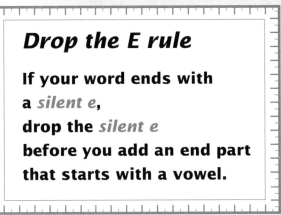

dinosaur

The Greek word *deinos* means *scary*.
The Greek word *sauros* means *lizard*.
So, a *scary lizard* is a *dinosaur*.

Trying out your spelling tools

1 — Your teacher will read a diary entry.
Listen. Finish the entry.

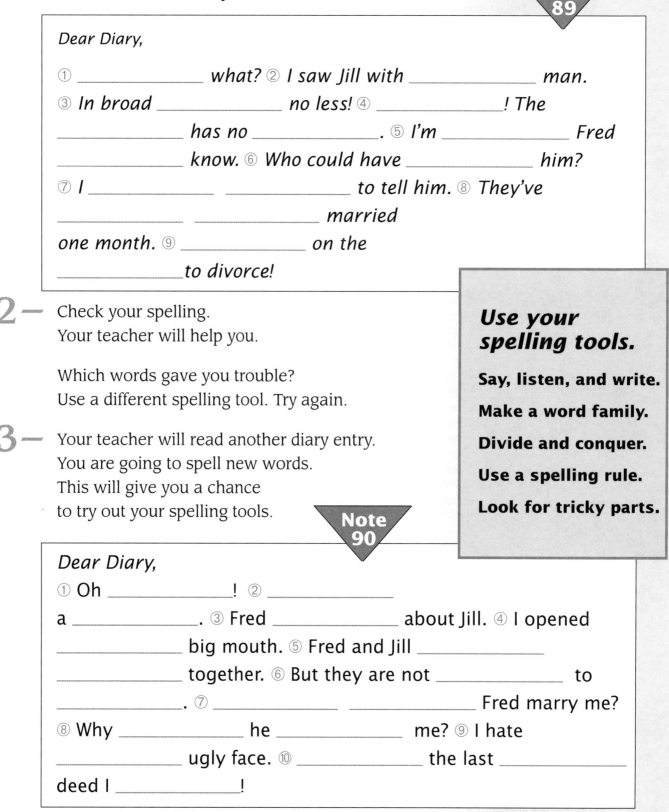

Note 89

Dear Diary,

① _____ what? ② I saw Jill with _____ man.
③ In broad _____ no less! ④ _____! The
_____ has no _____. ⑤ I'm _____ Fred
_____ know. ⑥ Who could have _____ him?
⑦ I _____ _____ to tell him. ⑧ They've
_____ _____ married
one month. ⑨ _____ on the
_____ to divorce!

2 — Check your spelling.
Your teacher will help you.

Which words gave you trouble?
Use a different spelling tool. Try again.

3 — Your teacher will read another diary entry.
You are going to spell new words.
This will give you a chance
to try out your spelling tools.

Note 90

Use your spelling tools.

Say, listen, and write.

Make a word family.

Divide and conquer.

Use a spelling rule.

Look for tricky parts.

Dear Diary,
① Oh _____! ② _____
a _____. ③ Fred _____ about Jill. ④ I opened
_____ big mouth. ⑤ Fred and Jill _____
_____ together. ⑥ But they are not _____ to
_____. ⑦ _____ _____ Fred marry me?
⑧ Why _____ he _____ me? ⑨ I hate
_____ ugly face. ⑩ _____ the last _____
deed I _____!

4— Check your spelling.
Your teacher will help you.

Which words gave you trouble?
Use a different spelling tool.
Try again.

Applying your spelling tools

1— Look at this example.

Slim did a good deed yesterday.
He writes about it
in his diary.

How did the deed turn out?

Dear Diary,
I had a bad, bad day.
The guy next door
has a cat.
(Or I should say
he had a cat.)
I gave the cat some
chicken bones.

I thought the cat would
like the bones.
But the cat choked.
It died.
I feel awful.

2— Your turn.

What did you do yesterday?

Write about it in your diary.

Dear Diary,

A final word

Which words about **Dear Diary**
would you like to add
to your dictionary?

Practice words

doing	surprise	just	super	suspect*
until	those	were	idea	everybody
clap	cheer	course	danced	dawn

*as in *They don't suspect a thing.*

Working with spelling tools

Say, listen, and write.

Say each word.
Listen to each sound.
Write the word as you say it.

super _____	suspect _____	clap _____
just _____	until _____	

If you say these words slowly,
you will have a good chance
of spelling them right.

Make a word family.

Say this word: **dawn**

Think of words that rhyme.
Write the words.
Your teacher will help you with the spelling.

Note
91

dawn

Look at your words.
Circle the words that belong
to the same word family as **dawn**.

Learn to spell one of these words, and
you will be able to spell all of the words.

Say this word: **cheer**

Think of words that rhyme.
Write the words.
Your teacher will help you with the spelling.

Note
92

cheer

Look at your words.
Circle the words that belong
to the same word family as **cheer**.

Learn to spell one of these words, and
you will be able to spell all of the words.

Say this word: **those**

Think of words that rhyme.
Write the words.
Your teacher will help you with the spelling.

Note
93

those

_____   _____   _____

_____   _____   _____

_____   _____   _____

_____   _____   _____

Look at your words.
Circle the words that belong
to the same word family as **those**.

Learn to spell one of these words, and
you will be able to spell all of the words.

Divide and conquer.

How can you divide and conquer
these words?

doing   _____
everybody _____
course   _____

> ### Divide and conquer
>
> **Do you see**
> ❏ **common beginning parts?**
> ❏ **common end parts?**
> ❏ **little words?**

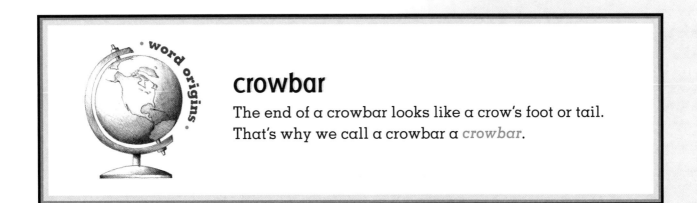

crowbar
The end of a crowbar looks like a crow's foot or tail.
That's why we call a crowbar a *crowbar*.

Use a spelling rule.

Practice the *Doubling* rule.

Say the base word.
Add the end part to the base word.
Say the new word.

clap + ing _____

clap + ed _____

clap + s _____

Doubling rule

If a word has ONE syllable and ends with ONE vowel and ONE consonant, double the final consonant when you add an end part that starts with a vowel.

Practice the *Y* rule (part 1).

Say the word.
Divide the word into two syllables.
Underline the letter that makes
the long **e** sound.

body _____

every _____

Y rule (part 1)

When you hear
the *long e* sound
at the end of a word
that has two syllables,
use *y.*

You have a good chance
of being right.

Y rule (part 2)

If a word ends in
consonant + y,
the *y* changes to *i*
when you add all end parts
except *ing.*

Practice the *Y* rule (part 2).

Say the base word.
Add the end part to the base word.
Say the new word.

body + s _____

Practice the *Silent E* rule.

Say the word.
Underline the long vowel sound.
Circle the silent **e**.

surprise	_____
those	_____

> ## Silent E rule
>
> **When you add the letter *e*
> to the end of a word,
> the short vowel sound
> in that word changes to
> a long vowel sound.**

Practice the *Drop the E* rule.

Say the base word.
Add the end part to the base word.
Say the new word.

surprise + ed	_____
surprise + ing	_____
surprise + is	_____
dance + er	_____
dance + ing	_____
dance + ed	_____
dance + s	_____
course + s	_____

> ## Drop the E rule
>
> **If your word ends with
> a *silent e*,
> drop the *silent e*
> before you add an end part
> that starts with a vowel.**

Look for tricky parts.

Look at the words below.
Look for the tricky parts.
Use the six steps to help you spell the words.

every	_____
surprise	_____
were	_____
idea	_____
course	_____

> ## Remember to . . .
>
> 1. **Read the word slowly.**
> 2. **Mark any tricky part.**
> 3. **Study the tricky part.**
> 4. **Cover the word.**
> 5. **Write the word.**
> 6. **Check the spelling.**

Trying out your spelling tools

1— Your teacher will read a thank you note.
Listen.
Finish the note.

▼ Note 94

Use your spelling tools.

Say, listen, and write.

Make a word family.

Divide and conquer.

Use a spelling rule.

Look for tricky parts.

Hi Sammy,
① *Thanks for* _____ *so much.* ② *The* _____ *party was* _____ . ③ _____ *banners* _____ *a great* _____ . ④ *My parents didn't* _____ *a thing.* ⑤ _____ *started to* _____ *and* _____ *when my parents walked into the hall.* ⑥ *I started to cry, of* _____ . ⑦ *We* _____ _____ _____ .

    Thanks again,
    Kim

2— Check your spelling.
Your teacher will help you.

Which words gave you trouble?
Use a different spelling tool. Try again.

debt

Why does the word *debt* have a *b* in it?
The word *debt* comes from the French word *dette*.
But a long time ago
smart people thought the word *debt*
came from the Latin word *debita*.
The smart people made a mistake,
and that's why we have to spell *debt* with a *b*.

word origins

3 — Your teacher will read another thank you note.
You are going to spell new words.
This will give you a chance
to try out your spelling tools.

Note 96

> Dearest Kim,
>
> ① _____ the _____! ② Your
> mother and I were so _____. ③ The
> _____ and _____. ④ And
> you and _____ Mom _____.
> ⑤ It was just _____ much! ⑥ _____ feet are sore
> from _____. ⑦ You _____ have worked
> _____ hard to plan the surprise (party). ⑧ We
> _____ forget it—_____!
>   Love,
>   Dad

Use your spelling tools.

Say, listen, and write.

Make a word family.

Divide and conquer.

Use a spelling rule.

Look for tricky parts.

4 — Check your spelling.
Your teacher will help you.

Which words gave you trouble?
Use a different spelling tool.
Try again.

Applying your spelling tools

1 — Look at this example.

You get a card in the mail.

This is what it says.

Hi!
I just wanted to say "thanks."
You have been great!
It was super working with you.
Your teacher.

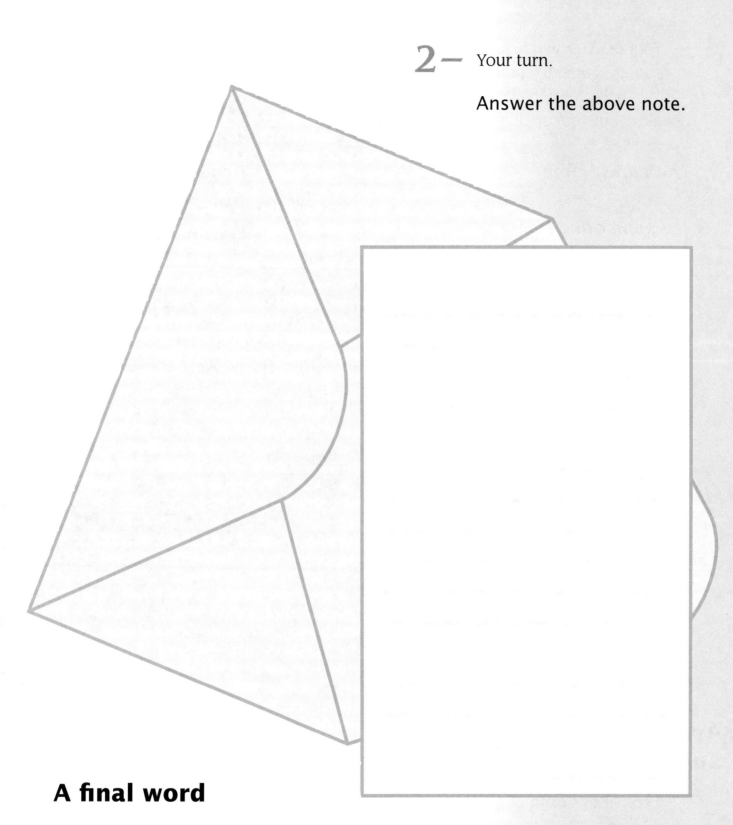

2— Your turn.

Answer the above note.

A final word

Which words about **notes**
would you like to add
to your dictionary?

Student Glossary

base word

A base word is a word that has no beginning parts or end parts.
Hat, **jump**, and **sun** are base words.
Hats, **jumped**, and **sunny** are not base words.

consonant

These letters are called consonants:
B   C   D   F   G   H   J   K   L   M
N   P   Q   R   S   T   V   W   X   Z
Sometimes **Y** is a consonant, too.

long vowel sounds

Long vowel sounds say their name.
The following words have long vowel sounds:
make   **Pete**   **bike**   **smoke**   **cute**

short vowel sounds

The following words have short vowel sounds:
tap   **pet**   **sit**   **pot**   **hut**

syllable

A syllable is a small part of a word.
Most of the time, a syllable has one vowel sound.
The following words all have two syllables:
Fri day   **bu sy**   **say ing**

vowel

The following letters are called vowels:
A   E   I   O   U
Sometimes, the letter **Y** is a vowel, too.

Word List

accept (10)
accident (15)
acts (8)
add (5)
address (6)
adults (9)
advice (14)
afternoon (2)
age (18)
ago (11)
alone (10)
along (14)
always (7)
ankle (15)
another (20)
apartment (5)
area (7)
argue (14)
arms (10)
around (8)
ask (19)
awful (14)
bad (14)
basement (6)
basketball (2)
because (6)
been (20)
began (11)
begin (17)
believe (18)
belong (7)
bigger (6)
bills (19)
binders (4)
black (15)

blue (15)
boil (16)
books(4)
born (18)
bowl (16)
breakfast (12)
brighter (6)
bring (19)
broken (15)
can't (20)
canned (16)
cast (15)
centre (7)
changes (18)
cheer (21)
children (9)
chilled (16)
chop (16)
clap (21)
cleaner (6)
close (5)
closed (10)
clothes (4)
coat (19)
complain (14)
completed (11)
contact (11)
contract (11)
course (21)
crutches (15)
cute (13)
damage (6)
danced (20)
dated (11)
daughter (3)

dawn (21)
daylight (20)
death (18)
deposit (6)
dice (16)
died (18)
doctor (15)
doesn't (20)
doing (21)
drag (12)
drier (6)
driver (11)
drop (19)
early (2)
easy (8)
elevator (6)
employed (11)
erasers (4)
every (12)
everybody (21)
everything (3)
exercise (17)
expecting (18)
facts (10)
family (3)
father (18)
favourite (7)
feel (8)
finally (13)
fire (14)
flab (17)
flat (3)
floor (5)
fly (3)
foil (19)

fool (12)
forget (9)
friendly (8)
frozen (16)
funny (13)
fussy (4)
gain (17)
garnish (16)
getting (3)
giggle (13)
glasses (19)
gone (18)
good-bye (6)
great (2)
gripe (14)
groan (13)
groups (7)
guess (20)
guys (12)
gym (17)
hang (2)
happening (7)
hardly (12)
healthy (9)
heard (13)
heart (18)
heating (6)
helping (8)
here's (13)
hide (14)
hire (5)
hobby (7)
honestly (20)
hospital (15)
hour (12)

house (2)
humdinger (13)
hungry (12)
hurry (3)
hurt (15)
idea (21)
ill (18)
interests (7)
invite (19)
jobs (10)
join (7)
just (21)
kind (8)
kitchen (5)
knock (5)
laps (17)
late (2)
lazy (17)
lease (6)
let's (9)
lift (17)
lined (4)
listen (7)
local (7)
lucky (9)
married (3)
maybe (14)
members (9)
might (13)
minds (10)
ministers (9)
miss (3)
mistake (14)
money (4)
mostly (12)
movie (2)
myself (12)
nap (2)
news (18)
newspaper (7)
night (2)

nobody (10)
notebooks (4)
November (11)
number (11)
O.K. (3)
October (11)
office (14)
only (20)
open (10)
order (2)
others (8)
out (2)
outside (5)
oven (16)
painting (5)
paper (4)
parents (9)
path (20)
pens (4)
permit (11)
person (8)
picky (4)
pizza (2)
place (9)
playing (17)
police (9)
posting (11)
presently (11)
problem (8)
punch (12)
quick (12)
quiet (2)
quite (14)
radio (7)
really (18)
repaper (5)
respect (14)
retile (5)
rich (9)
roll (19)
rulers (4)

runners (4)
said (13)
save (4)
saying (8)
serve (16)
shame (20)
shock (18)
short (3)
should (17)
silly (3)
simple (8)
sling (15)
smile (8)
soap (19)
someone (8)
something (7)
sometimes (12)
son-in-law (18)
sort (19)
sprained (15)
spring (3)
sprinkle (16)
stairs (6)
stand (10)
starving (12)
stiff (15)
story (10)
stove (16)
strained (15)
strange (13)
stretch (17)
strip (5)
strong (9)
stuff (4)
super (21)
sure (20)
surprise (21)
suspect (21)
switches (5)
table (5)
taste (16)

tbsp. (16)
teachers (9)
tell (10)
tennis (17)
that's (13)
there's (13)
they're (20)
those (21)
thought (13)
Thursday (19)
toilet (19)
told (20)
tone (17)
took (3)
toothpaste (19)
training (11)
trip (3)
true (10)
trust (10)
tsp. (16)
understand (10)
until (21)
usually (12)
varnish (5)
very (9)
wait (20)
washer (6)
watch (2)
wax (19)
weigh (17)
weight (17)
were (21)
what (13)
whine (14)
woman (20)
word (8)
x-rays (15)

Notes for Users

unit 1 • **introduction** • Spelling Tools

 Possible responses: bee, fee, gee, Lee, see, glee, knee, spree, tree, three / be, he, me, she, we / sea, tea, flea, plea / key / Chi, ski

Explain to the student that it is possible to have different spellings for the same sound; therefore, it's a good idea to learn words as groups or families, according to spelling.

 Spelling Rules

Doubling rule
If a word is one syllable and ends with one vowel and one consonant, double the final consonant when you add an end part that starts with a vowel.

Y rule
If a word has more than one syllable and ends with the long *e* sound, try using *y* for the long *e* sound.

If a word ends in consonant + *y*, the *y* changes to *i* when adding all suffixes, except *ing*. (If a word ends in vowel + *y*, there is no change when adding suffixes.)

Silent E rule
The short vowel sound becomes a long vowel sound in a CVC (consonant-vowel-consonant) word when *e* is added to the end of the word.

Drop the E rule
If a word ends in silent *e*, drop the *e* when adding a suffix that starts with a vowel. (Keep the *e* when adding a suffix that starts with a consonant.)

 Tricky Part
"Mark the tricky part" means highlight the part in some way (e.g., circling, underlining, highlighting with a marker, separating it off, etc.).

"Study the tricky part" can mean visualizing the part in some way, spelling it out loud, exaggerating the pronunciation, talking about how to remember it, etc.

 Tricky Part

breakfast–	You need two letters to make the short *e* sound.
crumb –	The letter *b* is silent.
class –	There are 2 *s*'s at the end of the word.
water –	The vowel *a* sounds like the short vowel *o*.

unit 2 • **home** • Leisure

 Possible responses: gout, lout, pout, rout, about, shout, snout, spout, stout, trout / doubt

Possible responses: fight, might, right, sight, tight, blight, bright, flight, fright, knight, plight, slight / bite, kite, lite, quite, sprite, trite, white, write / height

---

7 Possible responses: boon, goon, loon, moon, soon, croon, spoon / dune, June, tune

 8 Possible responses: douse, louse, mouse, souse, grouse

9 Dictation
1. I think (quiet) days are (great).
2. I like to (hang) around the (house).
3. I sleep (late). I don't get up (early).
4. I (watch) a (movie) in the (afternoon).
5. I like watching (basketball), too.
6. Sometimes, I (order) (pizza).
7. Then I take a (nap).
8. At (night), I go (out).

10 Dictation
1. (I'm) (so) busy now.
2. I work (afternoons) and (nights).
3. It's a (fight) to stay awake.
4. I (hate) these hours.
5. (It's) (about) time to (quit) this job.
6. I (might) go home early (tonight).

unit 3 • home • Family Times

 11 Possible responses: hiss, kiss, bliss / sis, this

 12 Possible responses: book, cook, hook, look, nook, rook, brook, crook, shook, mistook

 13 Possible responses: by, my, cry, dry, fry, try, why / dye, rye / die, lie, pie, tie / high, sigh / buy, guy / bye / hi / eye / aye

 14 Dictation
Hi Tammy!
1. How is (everything) with you?
2. Time sure does (fly).
3. How is the (family)?
4. We had an (O.K.) year.
5. Our (daughter) is (getting) (married).
6. Tom and I (took) a (short) (trip) in the (spring.)
7. We had five (flat) tires on the way.
8. We felt pretty (silly).
9. (Hurry) up and write!
10. We (miss) you.
Love,
 Brenda and Tom

15 Dictation
Hi guys!
1. You're right. Time really (flies).
2. The years seem to (get) (shorter).
3. I feel like (I'm) (hurrying) all the time.
4. How are the (marriage) plans going?
5. (My) sister (tripped) on the ice.
6. (She) hurt (her) (hip).
7. (She's) staying (with) (us) now.
8. Anyway, watch out for (flats)!
9. Hope to see you sometime (soon).
Tammy

unit 4 • home • Shopping

 16 Possible responses: cook, hook, look, nook, rook, took, brook, crook, shook, mistook

17 Possible responses: Dick, hick, kick, lick, Nick, Rick, sick, tick, wick, click, flick, prick, quick, slick, stick, trick / Bic, tic

Dictation
1. School (stuff) is pretty expensive.
2. I really have to (save) my (money).
3. My kids need (pens) and (books).
4. They need (binders) and (notebooks).
5. They need (rulers) and (erasers).
6. They need tons of (lined) (paper).
7. They always need new (clothes).
8. Things like (runners) aren't cheap.
9. And kids are so (fussy) and (picky).

 Dictation
1. (running) shoes
2. (clothing)
3. white (erasing) stuff
4. bathroom (hooks)
5. (shaving) foam
6. (wallpaper) and (sticky) paper

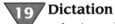 **unit 5 • home • Fix It Up**

 Possible responses: dock, hock, jock, lock, mock, rock, sock, block, clock, crock, frock, stock / gawk, hawk / talk, walk, chalk, stalk / wok

 Possible responses: faint, quaint, saint, taint, / ain't

Possible responses: itch, ditch, hitch, Mitch, pitch, witch, glitch, snitch, stitch / rich / niche

Possible responses: able, cable, fable, gable, sable, stable / label

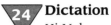 **Dictation**
Hi Val,
1. I rented that (apartment).
2. I'm (close) to a mall.
3. The (outside) hall needs (painting).
4. I have to wire the (switches).
5. I want to (knock) out a wall.
6. I want to (add) a fireplace.
7. I want to (repaper) the (kitchen).
8. I want to (strip) and (varnish) the (table).
9. I want to (hire) someone to (retile) the (floor).
What do you think?
Mitch

 Dictation
Hi Mitch,
1. (Installing) a fireplace! Wow!
2. I have (repapered) before.
3. (It's) messy work.
4. I have (stripped) and (varnished) (doors).
5. (I'm) good at it (now).
6. (Hiring) somebody is a (good) idea.
7. (How) about me?
8. (What) does the landlord think (about) (all) this?
Val

unit 6 • home • Changes

 Possible responses: bean, dean, jean, mean, wean, glean / keen, seen, teen, green, preen, queen, spleen / scene

Possible responses: fight, might, night, right, sight, tight, blight, flight, fright, knight, plight, slight / bite, kite, lite, quite, sprite, trite, white, write / height

 Possible responses: eat, beat, meat, neat, seat, cheat, treat, wheat / beet, feet, meet, fleet, greet, sheet, sleet, street / Pete

29 Dictation

Dear Manager,

1. I need to break my (lease) (because) this place is (too)cold.
2. I don't expect my (damage) (deposit) back.
3. My new place is (cleaner), (bigger) and (brighter).
4. The (elevator) works.
5. So, (good-bye) (stairs).
6. There's a (washer) and (drier) in the (basement).
7. The (heating) works.
8. I'm happy I have a new (address)!

Clair Tomlin Apt. 8

30 Dictation

Dear Manager,

1. (This) apartment is not good.
2. I spent (two) weeks (cleaning) it.
3. The elevator is still (busted).
4. I have to climb ten (flights) of stairs!
5. I (had) to buy a (heater).
6. The floors (are) (damaged).
7. The (downstairs) is full of water.
8. What a (dive)! (Why) me!
9. I was better off (with) my old place.

Clair Tomlin
Apt. 2

unit 7 • community • Things to do

31 Dictation

1. What's happening in your town?
2. Do you have a (favourite) (hobby)?
3. What are your (interests)?
4. Do you (belong) to any (groups)?
5. (Join) a (local) rec (centre).
6. Check the (newspaper).
7. (Listen) to the (radio).
8. They tell you what's (happening) in your (area).
9. There's (always) (something) to do.

32 Dictation

1. My (friend) loves movies.
2. He (joined) a (movie) (club).
3. (He) (loves) it!
4. He (said) it's very (interesting).
5. (They) go on trips (sometimes).
6. Maybe (I'll) join the club.
7. I don't have (many) (hobbies).
8. (But) anyone (can) watch a movie.

unit 8 • community • Action

33 Possible responses: bound, found, hound, mound, pound, round, sound, ground / clowned (around), renowned

34 Possible responses: dimple, pimple

35 Possible responses: eel, heel, keel, kneel, peel, reel, steel / deal, heal, meal, real, seal, teal, veal, zeal, steal / Neil / spiel

36 Possible responses: mother, brother, another

37 Dictation

1. (Helping) (others) is (easy).
2. Look (around).
3. Is there (someone) who needs help?
4. A (friendly) (smile) is good.
5. (Saying) a (kind) (word) is good, too.
6. Listen to a friend's (problem).
7. These are (simple) (acts).
8. They make people (feel) good.
9. One (person) can make a difference.

38 Dictation

1. I (helped) at the bingo last (night).
2. It (was) (easier) than I thought.
3. I (had) to (call) out (winning) cards.
4. I left the place (smiling).
5. I have (found) (something) I like to do.
6. My (friend) (says) she wants to help, (too).

The Spelling Toolbox ■ **Workbook 2**

unit 9 • community • Relations

 Possible responses: each, beach, peach, reach, bleach, breach, preach / beech, leech, beseech

 Possible responses: buck, duck, muck, puck, suck, tuck, yuck, chuck, cluck, pluck, shmuck, shuck, stuck, struck, truck / yuk

 Possible responses: ace, face, lace, mace, pace, race, grace, trace / base, case, vase, chase

 Dictation
Dear Community Readers,
1. We have a (strong), (healthy) community.
2. I thank many community (members) for this.
3. Our (police) and our (ministers).
4. Our (teachers) and our (parents).
5. Our (children) and young (adults).
6. We're (very) (lucky).
7. Let's not (forget) how (lucky) we are.
8. (Let's) keep this a great (place) to live.
Andrew Dobbs
Editor

 Dictation
Dear Community Readers,
1. We are losing a (member) of (our) community.
2. Carmen Chen is off to new (places).
3. (She's) going to Africa to (teach).
4. (We'll) miss her.
5. Our community is (richer) because of (her).
6. Don't stay (away) too (long), Carmen!
7. Best (wishes) (from) us all.
Andrew Dobbs Editor

unit 10 • community • Changes

 Possible responses: bell, fell, hell, Nell, sell, well, yell, shell, smell, spell, swell / gel, Mel

 Dictation
Dear Mayor:
Who are these new people in our city?
1. We need to (understand).
2. Do these people want our (jobs)?
3. Should we (open) our (arms) to them?
4. Should we (accept) and (trust) them?
5. We don't want (closed) (minds).
6. But, (nobody) will (tell) us the (facts)!
7. That's why I'm taking a (stand).
8. I want the (true) (story).
9. Am I (alone) on this?
Signed
Jean Begin

 Dictation
Dear Jean Begin:
Regarding your letter to the mayor:
1. A (new) (family) lives next door.
2. They're (from) Spain.
3. We (opened) our arms to (them).
4. They (trusted) us.
5. (Do) they want to take (our) jobs?
6. Should we (listen) to rumours and (stories)?
7. I (don't) know.
8. I just know (we're) friends.
Signed
A neighbour

unit 11 • work • Forms

Possible responses: gain, pain, rain, vain, drain, grain, plain, sprain, stain, strain / bane, cane, Dane, Jane, lane, mane, pane, sane, vane, crane, plane / deign, feign, reign / Wayne

Dictation
1. I saw your job (posting) (dated) (November) 1.
2 It was asking for a (driver).
3. I (began) a course one year (ago).
4. I (completed) my (training) in (October).
5. I have my (permit).
6. I am (presently) (employed).
7. My (contract) ends this month.
8. Please (contact) me at this (number).

49 **Dictation**
1. I (saw) your ad dated (September) 9.
2. The (post) interests me.
3. I will (complete) my (present) contract in October.
4. I will then be (unemployed).
5. I (have) the (permits) you need.
6. Please contact (me) at (these) (numbers).
7. I (look) forward (to) hearing (from) you.

50 **Apply Speling Tools**
dog-walker

unit 12 • work • Routines

51 **Possible responses:** Dick, hick, kick, lick, Nick, pick, Rick, sick, tick, wick, click, flick, prick, slick, stick, trick / Bic, tic

52 **Possible responses:** cool, pool, tool, drool, school, spool, stool / ghoul / jewel / rule, Yule / who'll, you'll / duel, cruel, gruel

53 **Dictation**
1. I work in a shop.
2. I (punch) in (every) morning.
3. (Sometimes), I eat a (quick) (breakfast).
4. But (usually), I'm not (hungry).
5. (Mostly) I keep to (myself).

6. I (hardly) talk to the other (guys).
7. They're O.K. They (fool) around a lot.
8. By lunch (hour), I'm (starving).
9. After lunch, the time can (drag).

54 **Dictation**
1. (Most) jobs are (good) and bad.
2. (Some) jobs are (hard).
3. You need a lot of (school).
4. But the (pay) is (very) good.
5. (Other) jobs are (easy).
6. (But) the pay is lousy.
7. Or the job is (boring).
8. You (can't) have (everything).

unit 13 • work • Memo Board

55 **Possible responses:** fight, light, night, right, sight, tight, blight, bright, flight, fright, knight, plight, slight / bite, kite, quite, sprite, trite, white, write / height

56 **Possible responses:** ought, bought, fought, sought, brought / caught, naught, taught, fraught / cot, dot, got, hot, jot, lot, not, pot, rot, sot, tot, clot, knot, plot, shot, slot, snot, spot, trot / yacht

57 **Possible responses:** jiggle, wiggle, squiggle, wriggle

58 **Dictation**
1. (Thought) this (might) give you a (giggle).
2. (Heard) this (humdinger) the other day.
3. This will make you (groan).
4. Too (cute), eh?
5. Too (funny), eh?
6. (Here's) a good one.
7. (There's) this guy . . .
8. She (said), "(What)?"
9. He (finally) says . . .
10. (That's) a (strange) one, eh?

Dictation
1. Here's a (funnier) one.
2. Here are a few (giggles) for you.
3. These are the (cutest) (stories)!
4. Here's a (groaner).
5. (That's) a (sight) for sore eyes!
6. (This) has got to be the (strangest)!
7. (These) (are) my favourite (sayings).
8. I've (seen) (everything) now!

unit 14 • **work** • Relations

 Dictation
Help me Beatrice!
1. This job was a (bad) (mistake).
2. All we do is (whine) and (complain).
3. The bosses (hide) in their (office).
4. They (gripe) and (argue).
5. There's no (respect).
6. It's (quite) (awful).
7. Nobody gets (along).
8. (Maybe) they'll (fire) me.
9. Any (advice)?
Miss you awfully,
Spike

 Dictation
Hi Spike
1. The job sounds (awfully) bad.
2. And (your) bosses (sound) worse!
3. (Hiding) in their (offices).
4. (Griping) and (arguing).
5. What's (wrong) with (them)?
6. Hang in (there) (until) Christmas.
7. Then maybe you (should) quit.
Beatrice

unit 15 • **health** • General

 Possible responses: gain, pain, rain, vain, drain, grain, plain, stain, train / bane, cane, Dane, Jane, lane, mane, pane, sane, vane, crane, plane / deign, feign, reign / Wayne

 Possible responses: back, hack, jack, lack, pack, rack, sack, tack, whack, clack, crack, flack, knack, quack, slack, snack, stack, track / Mac / yak

 Possible responses: Dutch, hutch, clutch / much, such / touch

 Dictation
Suzy!
What happened?
1. (Slings), (casts) and crutches! Oh my!
2. How's (your) (back)?
3. How's (Ted's) ankle?
4. Your dad (broke) (his) finger.
5. (They) put a (splint) on it.
6. You (know) how he hates (doctors) and (hospitals).
7. He (didn't) want to go.
8. (Boy)! When it (rains), it pours.
9. Keep me (posted) on what's (happening).
Mom

unit 16 • **health** • Diet

 Possible responses: oil, coil, foil, soil, toil, broil, spoil / loyal, royal

 Possible responses: crinkle, tinkle, winkle, twinkle, wrinkle

Possible responses: ice, lice, mice, nice, rice, vice, price, slice, splice, twice, advice, entice

 Dictation
1. Heat (oven) to 350°F.
2. (Boil) water on (stove).
3. Add 2 (tsp.) pepper and salt.
4. (Dice) and (chop) fruit.
5. Add (frozen) peas to (bowl).
6. Mix in (canned) corn.
7. Add 1 (tbsp.) butter.
8. (Sprinkle) with sugar to (taste).
9. (Garnish) with mint.
10. (Serve) with (chilled) drinks.

Dictation
1. Put 2 (cans) of corn in a (mixing)* bowl.
2. (Mix) in a (can) of peas.
3. Add one (diced) cucumber.
4. (Add) some (chopped) green onion.
5. Mix in 1/2 (cup) of Italian dressing.
6. (Chill) for one (hour).
7. Garnish with (slices) of tomato.
8. (Serves) 6 as a side (dish).

*Do not use the *Doubling* rule with the letter *x*. You never see *xx* in English spelling.

unit 17 • health • Fitness

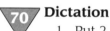 **Possible responses:** main, pain, rain, vain, drain, grain, plain, sprain, stain, strain, train / bane, cane, Dane, Jane, lane, mane, pane, sane, vane, crane, plane, inane, insane / deign, feign, reign / Wayne / Maine

 Possible responses: could, would / good, hood, wood, stood

Possible responses: etch, fetch, retch, vetch, wretch

 Dictation
I'm so (lazy).
1. I (should) (exercise) more.
2. I need to (stretch) and (tone).
3. I'm all (flab).
4. I don't want to (gain) (weight).
5. I'm afraid to (weigh) myself.
6. I'll start (playing) (tennis).
7. I'll (lift) weights.
8. I'll run (laps). I'll join a (gym).
9. I'll (begin) tomorrow!

 Dictation
1. (Tomorrow) (has) come and gone.
2. So much for (exercising).
3. Good-bye (stretching) and (toning).
4. Hello (flabby) body.
5. I (would) exercise (more).
6. I just (don't) have the time.
7. (I'll) buy some (weights) at Christmas.
8. I'll (start) (training) in the new year.
9. Come (rain) (or) (shine)!

unit 18 • health • Changes

 Possible responses: dill, fill, gill, hill, Jill, kill, mill, pill, sill, till, will, chill, drill, frill, grill, quill, shrill, skill, spill, still, swill, thrill, trill / Lil, nil, until

Possible responses: dock, hock, jock, lock, mock, rock, sock, block, clock, crock, frock, knock, stock / gawk, hawk / talk, walk, chalk, stalk / wok

Dictation

Merry Christmas Lucy!
1. There is lots of (news).
2. There have been many (changes).
3. My (father) (died). It was his (heart).
4. He was (really) (ill).
5. Still, his (death) was a (shock).
6. He lived to a good old (age).
7. But, I can't (believe) he's (gone).
8. I have a new (son-in-law).
9. My daughter is (expecting).
10. The baby will be (born) in July.

Take care,
Helga

 Dictation

Hi Helga. Merry Christmas!
1. So sorry to hear (about) your dad.
2. Life (always) brings (change).
3. (Your) dad (was) a good man.
4. I'm (still) in London.
5. I (expect) to be here for (ages).
6. My (sister) lives (here) now, too.
7. It's (real) nice having her here.
8. Other than that, (nothing) (new).

Send pictures of the baby next year.
Lucy

unit 19 • writings • Lists

 Possible responses: oil, boil, coil, soil, toil, broil, spoil / loyal, royal

 Possible responses: ass, bass, lass, mass, pass, sass, class, crass, grass / gas

 Possible responses: oat, boat, goat, moat, bloat, float, gloat, throat / dote, note, quote, rote, tote, vote, wrote

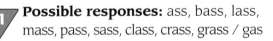 **Possible responses:** ill, dill, fill, gill, hill, Jill, kill, mill, pill, sill, till, will, chill, drill, frill, grill, quill, shrill, skill, spill, still, swill, thrill, trill / Lil, nil, until

 Dictation
1. Get (toothpaste), (toilet) paper, one (roll) (wax) paper (foil) wrap, hand (soap).
2. (Bring) in (glasses).
3. (Sort) out (bills).
4. (Ask) Suni about work stuff.
5. (Invite) Leo for (Thursday).
6. (Drop) off Mom's (coat).

 Dictation

I've already . . .
1. (dropped) (off) Mom's coat
2. (sorted) out bills
3. (invited) Leo for Thursday
4. (asked) Suni (about) work

I still have to . . .
5. (fax) (stuff) to work
6. (fix) (dad's) glasses
7. pick up (rolled) (oats) (for) mom
8. (pay) water (bill)

 Apply Spelling Tools
circus manager

unit 20 • writings • Dear Diary

Possible responses: mother, brother, another, smother

Possible responses: fight, might, night, right, sight, tight, blight, bright, flight, fright, knight, plight, slight / bite, kite, quite, sprite, trite, white, write / height

Dictation

Dear Diary
1. (Guess) what?
2. I saw Jill with (another) man!
3. In broad (daylight) no less!
4. (Honestly)! The (woman) has no (shame).
5. I'm (sure) Fred (doesn't) know.
6. Who could have (told) him?
7. I (can't) (wait) to tell him.
8. They've (only) (been) married one month.
9. (They're) on the (path) to divorce!

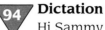

90 ▼ **Dictation**
Dear Diary
Oh (brother)!
1. (What) a (night).
2. Fred (guessed) about Jill.
3. I opened (my) big mouth.
4. Fred and Jill (are) (still) together.
5. But they're not (talking) to (me).
6. (Why) (didn't) Fred marry me?
7. Why (does) he (blame) me?
8. I hate (his) ugly face.
9. (That's) the last (good) deed I (do)!

unit 21 • writings • Notes

91 ▼ **Possible responses:** fawn, lawn, pawn, yawn, brawn, prawn, spawn / on, con, Don, non, Ron, upon / gone / wan, swan / John / Sean / Shaun

92 ▼ **Possible responses:** beer, deer, jeer, leer, peer, seer, veer, queer, sneer, steer / ear, dear, fear, gear, hear, near, rear, tear, year, clear, smear, spear / pier, tier / here, mere / we're

93 ▼ **Possible responses:** chose, close, hose, nose, pose, rose, prose, suppose / bows, lows, mows, rows, tows, blows, crows, flows, glows, grows, knows, shows, slows, snows, stows, throws / doze, froze / does, foes, goes, hoes, toes, woes, floes / Joe's

94 ▼ **Dictation**
Hi Sammy,
1. Thanks for (doing) so much.
2. The (surprise) party was (just) (super).
3. (Those) banners (were) a great (idea).
4. My parents didn't (suspect) a thing.
5. (Everybody) started to (clap) and (cheer) when my parents walked into the hall.
6. I started to cry, of (course).
7. We (danced) (until) (dawn).
Thanks again,
Kim

95 ▼ **Dictation**
Dearest Kim,
1. (You're) the (best)!
2. Your mother and I were so (surprised).
3. The (clapping) and (cheering).
4. And you and (your) mom (crying).
5. It was just (too) much!
6. (Our) feet are sore from (dancing).
7. You (must) have worked (so) hard to plan the surprise (party).
8. We (won't) forget it—(ever)!
Love,
Dad